STEFAN BUCOVINEANUL-VOLOSENIUC

Just Imagine

Stefan Bucovineanul-Voloseniuc

Copyright © 2024 Stefan Bucovineanul-Voloseniuc

The moral right of the author has been asserted.

Apart from any fair dealing for the purposes of research or private study, or criticism or review, as permitted under the Copyright, Designs and Patents Act 1988, this publication may only be reproduced, stored or transmitted, in any form or by any means, with the prior permission in writing of the publishers, or in the case of reprographic reproduction in accordance with the terms of licences issued by the Copyright Licensing Agency. Enquiries concerning reproduction outside those terms should be sent to the publishers.

Matador
Unit E2 Airfield Business Park
Harrison Road, Market Harborough
Leicestershire LE16 7UL
Tel: 0116 279 2299
Email: books@troubador.co.uk
Web: www.troubador.co.uk/matador
Twitter: @matadorbooks

ISBN 978 1805142 072

British Library Cataloguing in Publication Data.
A catalogue record for this book is available from the British Library.

Printed and bound by CPI Group (UK) Ltd, Croydon, CR0 4YY
Typeset in 11pt Minion Pro by Troubador Publishing Ltd, Leicester, UK

Matador is an imprint of Troubador Publishing Ltd

STEFAN BUCOVINEANUL-VOLOSENIUC
Just Imagine

To Simona, my steadfast ally and dearest friend, and to our four incredible children.
Also, to my mother, an extraordinary woman to whom we owe immeasureable gratitude.

CONTENTS

	Foreword	ix
1	Arrival	1
2	Rural Romania	3
3	My Father	8
4	Growing Up	33
5	Portugal	73
6	Paris	93
7	London	99
8	Business Beginnings	111
9	Simona	128
10	My First Business	140
11	The Business of Business	153
12	Other Ventures	177
13	Politics	184
14	New Challenges	199
15	Giving Back	208
16	Romania Today	213
17	Reflections and the Future	223

FOREWORD

A lot of this book is based on my memory and the recollections of family and friends who have also kindly contributed theirs as well.

When I was growing up in a small house in a remote village in Northern Romania during the years that followed the 1989 revolution, the emphasis was more on survival and secrecy than art or literature.

Ours was not a house of books or writing and we didn't keep diaries so I have little written information from my childhood or early years, but fortunately there is a lot more from recent times thanks to my work records, social media and my wife Simona's organisation and attention to detail.

I've tried to be as accurate as possible but know that even though many of these events were only a few decades ago, the memory and mind can sometimes play strange tricks.

But this is how I remember my life and my story and I hope that I've got the names, dates and details right!

1

Arrival

'Hello Iacob it's Stefan, I landed and came through customs much faster than I expected.'

'Hey Stefan, that's great, welcome to the UK! What time train are you getting? I'll come and meet you at Victoria Station.'

'I'm not sure yet but I'm in the queue for a taxi to Glasgow Airport Station so can tell you when I get there.'

'You mean Gatwick Airport Station, but you shouldn't need a taxi to get there as the trains come straight into the airport.'

'No, it says Glasgow on all the signs. G.L.A.S.G.O.W.'

There was a brief silence on the other end of the phone.

'You can't be in Glasgow – why would you be in Glasgow?!'

'I got the plane here from Paris as it was cheap. I thought that was a good thing to do to save some money?'

'Stefan, Glasgow is in Scotland, a completely different country and about 400 miles from London which is where I'm waiting for you!'

There was another silence, this time from me.

'I guess that's not good. Sorry. What should I do now?'

'You'd better go to that station and get a train towards London.'

That was my first conversation in the UK, as a 24-year-old man from a tiny and very poor village in the forests of Northern Romania, and it hadn't gone quite as smoothly as I'd hoped.

It was the spring of 2007 and I spoke no English but had just arrived (in the wrong place!) to look for a job, find a home and start a new life, all with only a borrowed £200 in my wallet.

Unfortunately, geography had never been my best subject at school and I had assumed that as Glasgow was in the UK it was probably near to London!

Not for the first time I was to discover that I had a lot to learn, but I was at the start of a truly incredible journey that has brought me a lot of happiness and a wonderful family and many amazing experiences.

2

Rural Romania

There is a 20-minute film on YouTube called *Radu, boy of Romania* that was produced by film-makers Andre Waksman and Arnold Baskin. It tells the story of a young boy, Radu, who lives in the Northern Romanian commune of Bogdan Voda, less than two hours' drive from the village of Cârlibaba where I spent most of my early years.

The film portrays what seems to be an almost mediaeval lifestyle where the clothes are basic and traditional and still washed by hand in the river. They are made by the local women who cut and soak the hemp before drying it on the wooden fences that surround each home. They then separate the fibres so they can spin and weave them into clothing on their home looms.

The people are clearly very poor but do own their houses, which are mainly small, wooden and functional.

The villages are surrounded by the forests where most of the men work, and use horses and carts and traditional tools to fell the trees.

We see how the older people still contribute in a wide variety of ways, whether in the fields, spinning wool, looking after their grandchildren or teaching and passing on local traditions. The children also get up at dawn to do their own chores, which include sweeping, cutting wood and feeding animals before heading to school in their bare feet.

Life revolves around the rhythms of the river and the forest. In the spring, the shepherds take their sheep and cows to the higher mountain pastures where they make their own cheese.

To do this, they milk the cows, separate the curd, and then hang it in linen cloth bundles to dry in the sun. This is a life where almost everything is done by hand and by the people themselves.

The community divides up the land, which is collectivised and owned by the state. Each farmer is allocated a certain area to cultivate in return for a share of the harvest.

Blacksmiths are very important, as there are more than 200 horses in the village, and wheelmakers are also crucial since wagons are the main form of transport. Vets are as important as doctors in a rural community like this.

The film shows us that there are very few shops in the village. Gypsy caravans are the main source for purchasing pots and pans and other essential household items when they are passing through.

Food in the evening is basic and repetitive. It consists

largely of bean soup, bread, pickled cucumbers and mamaliga – also known as polenta – which is one of the main local specialities. Made of ground cornmeal, it can be mixed with milk, cheese or lard, and is a nourishing and cheap dish for families.

Sunday church services are very important to the villagers, as they are one of the few times when people can take a break from work and spend time together. On Sundays, everyone wears their embroidered leather and sheepskin jackets. We see women in their colourful headscarves, walking and talking and meeting friends and neighbours.

It is a very hard life, but responsibility comes naturally to the villagers because there is a lot of work to do and they have no choice but to rely on themselves and their children.

Are you wondering when this film was made? Is it perhaps capturing life at the turn of the 20th Century when cameras were first visiting the more remote regions of Europe? Or is it actually a reconstruction of a mediaeval village for a TV drama or feature film?

No. It was made in 1971 at a time when the Apollo 14 landed men on the moon for the third time, Disney World opened in Florida, Intel released the world's first microprocessor and across Europe the citizens of our neighbouring countries were enjoying international holidays and watching global sporting events on colour televisions. Those European consumers had a wide range of options available for items they took for granted – such as cars, washing machines, fridges and clothes.

And yet, Romanians were still living under a brutal

communist dictatorship, with a megalomaniac leader whose visits to North Korea and China that year saw him develop a taste for an ever-greater personality cult.

Every day was spent in fear of Nicolae Ceausescu's sinister network of secret police, the Securitate. Even close friends and neighbours came under suspicion of being informers. Romanians were obsessed with secrecy because they knew that information gathered about them could lead to evictions, job loses, school bans, blackmail or jail. It really was that bad.

In all parts of Romania, the souls of the people were beaten down by authoritarian communism as its endless, mindless, pointless bureaucracy strangled ideas and any small attempts at innovation. Corruption suppressed the rare outbreaks of civil spirit and led to a passive acceptance of suffering and a slavish obedience to authority figures, just so that people could protect their families and survive in what was little more than a day-by-day existence.

And this was a film that was made just 12 years before I was born, in 1983.

It is incredible to think that this was how my parents and grandparents lived, and how similar our lives in Cârlibaba still were to Radu and his family when I was a young child. It is also difficult for my friends in London to appreciate just how bad the poverty really was, and the way our mothers had to spend many hours each week standing in long lines for meat, bread and fruit.

Food was rationed, along with electricity, heating and gas, because most of what was produced was taken by the government and sold abroad to pay Ceausescu's debts. It was no wonder so many millions of young Romanians left the country as soon as they were able, to seek a better life elsewhere and send money home to support their families.

I was one of them. Coming to live and work in England has proved to be the best decision I could have made, as it has provided me with a life and security that my parents and grandparents could never even have dreamed about.

This book is the story of how it all happened – the many challenges and obstacles I faced, the successes and failures, the creation of my businesses, and a reflection on what I have learned during my first four decades.

3

My Father

On October 15, 2020, I had a phone call from my mother to say that my father didn't have long to live and was asking for me to come home and see him. I managed to get a flight from London to Cluj the following evening and hired a car to drive the 200km to their home in Cârlibaba.

Arriving the next morning, I went straight to his bedside. After his very long and difficult battle with cancer, my father could no longer speak, but he was able to see me and make some small gestures. Along with other members of our family, we spent his final few hours together.

Three days after I received that call, Ilie Voloseniuc died at 5.30pm. He was 77. My younger brother Ilie and I sat with him at his bedside, telling him that we loved him and that it was ok for him to go. We held and stroked his hands as he lay silently in bed, his body ravaged by cancer.

He was no more than the shell of the man I had spent so much of my life struggling to understand.

My mother, Maria, his wife of 39 years, silently watched him leave us. As I gently wiped a tear from his left eye, his breathing stopped and an often unhappy life that had seen him face many challenges and difficulties was finally, peacefully closed.

The defining relationship of my life was with my father, but it was rarely an easy one as he was often a distant and remote man. He was very, very tough and it was hard to be his son, especially his eldest one. I didn't always know how to connect with him. It often seemed there was something very cold between us, and that was sad as it had a direct impact on so much else that has happened in my life.

It was only really in his final months that I felt as though I began to understand him. He relented slightly, reluctantly allowing his children to enter his private world and take care of him. When we realised that, despite all the treatments and medical visits, my dad had very little time left, I took several weeks off work in London in the summer of 2020 so that my family and I could spend time with my parents in their home village. We walked and talked together in the beautiful woods and mountains I had known and loved as a boy.

It was a very precious period that I'm so glad we had, especially as it meant that my three children were able to get to know their grandparents. They now have many wonderful photographs to remind them about that time, which they will be able to look back on when they are older.

Shortly before he died, my father told me that he loved me. It was the first time in my life he'd said that, and I was immensely moved, but also very heavy-hearted that it had taken the knowledge that he didn't have much longer to live before he could finally say those words to me.

As a parent myself, I know how strong my own feelings are towards my children, and I try to be an open and loving father who shows them emotional support. My own dad was never able to do that, which was very sad.

I do, however, now have a better and more empathetic understanding of his own background and childhood, and have learned how his early experiences forged the man I knew. There are many examples of how political decisions taken in Bucharest during and after World War II had a great – and perhaps unintended – impact on the people who lived many hundreds of miles away. The butterfly effect was never more real than in Romania during that period.

Ilie came into the world during that terrible war on July 13, 1943. He was born in Izvoarele Sucevei – a small commune consisting of three villages on the border with Ukraine. The population was split fairly evenly between Ukrainians and Romanians.

His parents, Stefan and Teodora, were from families who had lived in the area for many generations. Their home was surrounded by forests and mountains, much the same as today, and life was very basic.

He was one of nine children, but despite having such a large family he always seemed to be an outsider and a loner, and wasn't very close to any of them. My uncle Petre once told me that his brother's distance may have been explained by a family rumour that he might have been the illegitimate son of a German soldier.

The unconfirmed story was that, when my grandfather was away from home fighting in the Romanian army, a group of German soldiers came through the village. They were always euphemistically described as having 'visited' the local women – including, so it was rumoured, my grandmother. But, in reality, it sounds as though the women were given little or no choice about whether or not they could reject any physical advances from the visitors.

Nine months later, my father was born, and the subject was forbidden from ever being discussed. While researching this book, I've looked at photos of him and his family and it does seem that my father looks different to the rest of his siblings. But it is not something I ever felt able to speak to him about, even though it potentially has a direct impact on my identity as well.

As I have grown older, I have been able to view Romania from the outside and learn an alternative version of the limited and tightly controlled history of our nation that was presented to us at school. As a result, I feel I have a far greater knowledge of what my father had lived through, and why he took the approach to life that he did – especially as he grew up amid the turmoil that almost destroyed Romania in the years immediately after the end of the war.

It must have been an incredibly confusing and stressful time for my family, as they were so close to the Soviet border. Impartial information and news would have been scarce and unreliable. In order to give some context to their story and the world my dad grew up in, I think it is useful to briefly share a few of the key Romanian events and personalities of that dreadful period in our nation's history, as they ultimately had a huge influence on his life – and, through him, on mine.

Romania is a nation whose borders have fluctuated on a regular basis for many centuries, but is made up of three main and distinct regions: Transylvania in the west, Moldavia in the east and Wallachia in the south. It currently has borders with Moldova, Ukraine, Hungary, Serbia and Bulgaria, and a small coastline on the Black Sea.

Officially neutral under King Carol II, the then Kingdom of Romania was initially determined to stay out of the impending war. Gradually, however, because the country was in such a key strategic position between Russia and the Balkan states, it was drawn into the conflict.

When World War II broke out on September 1, 1939 it declared neutrality. But that did little to protect the nation from the growing conflict and in June 1940, Russia invaded the north–eastern regions of Bessarabia and Bucovina.

Carol responded by installing a far-right government under Ion Gigurtu and anti-semitism became official government policy. Jews were banned from public office, the legal profession and the military – and from marrying Romanians – as the nation slid towards an increasingly dark future.

Those moves failed to satisfy the German leader Adolf Hitler. Yet further cuts were made into the map of Romania when Hitler and his Italian ally Benito Mussolini apportioned Northern Transylvania to Hungary, and Southern Dobrogea to Bulgaria.

This meant that one third of the territory established as Greater Romania in the treaties signed at the end of World War I had suddenly been lost. As had happened so often during its long and troubled history, Romania's borders and people were being moved unilaterally, and against their wishes.

In September, after just two months in office, Gigurtu resigned. The King gave in to intense military and political pressure by dissolving parliament, suspending the constitution, and handing General Ion Antonescu full dictatorial powers. He then abdicated, and handed the throne to his 18-year-old son Michael before leaving the country.

A few weeks later, Romania officially – and inevitably – entered the war on the side of Germany and the Axis powers, with Antonescu committing a vast Romanian army to take part in the campaign against Russia.

In June 1944, after four years of devastating bloodshed and increasing poverty, opposition parties joined together as the NDB (National Democratic Bloc), and told King Michael and the Allies that they wanted to withdraw from the war and negotiate a peace.

On August 23, the NDB formed a government and an armistice with the allies was announced. General Antonescu was arrested and later executed. It is estimated that more than 600,000 Romanians had been killed, wounded or were listed as missing as a result of the war.

The country's economy had been utterly devastated by the conflict, but this was only the beginning. We were about to lurch into an even longer period when the people had little say in their lives and destiny.

Romania was now on the side of the Allies, but yet again lost control of its borders when a secret Moscow conference in October 1944 divided the nations of Eastern Europe into spheres of influence. The decisions were taken by the British prime minister Winston Churchill and the Russian leader Joseph Stalin, with the full agreement of the Americans.

In return for gaining 90 per cent influence in Greece, the British agreed to give the same deal to the Soviets in Romania, as it was such an important buffer state on their border. The territories and control of Bulgaria, Hungary and Yugoslavia were also allocated in what became known as the Percentages Agreement, after the piece of paper that Stalin had written his demands on.

Romania was forced to sign an armistice with the Soviet Union on behalf of the Allies, and although Northern Transylvania was returned, the Soviets took almost complete political and economic control over the entire country.

Amidst the post-war turmoil, elections were held on November 19, 1946. They resulted in a controversial win for the communist-dominated BDP and Dr Petru Groza, who was widely viewed as being little more than a Soviet-backed puppet prime minister.

For the first time, a communist-controlled government was in charge of Romania. While the attention of Western Europe was focused on rebuilding their own shattered nations, Romanian opposition leaders were arrested and killed, and a series of new laws were introduced to centralise control of the economy and property.

The peace treaty was eventually signed in Paris on February 10, 1947. It resulted in yet another redrawing of the map with an agreement that restored Romania only to its borders of January 1, 1941.

Even this came with some major concessions in return for the Russian army finally leaving the country. The Soviet Union kept control of Bessarabia and Northern Bucovina, and Bulgaria annexed Southern Dobrogea, while Romania was also ordered to pay 300 million US dollars in reparations to the Soviet Union.

The next key event came on December 30, 1947, when King Michael was forced to abdicate shortly after returning home from attending the wedding of his cousins Princess Elizabeth and Prince Philip in Westminster Abbey in London.

The Romanian People's Republic was proclaimed, and the communists set about creating a Stalinist Soviet model of society with even more central controls imposed on the economy, media, military, culture and heritage. All religions except the Orthodox church were banned, and even that was subject to strong control by the government.

The Congress of the Communist Party decreed that the Romanian Workers' Party would become the only legal political organisation, with Gheorghe Gheorghiu-Dej as general secretary. The dreaded Directorate of the People's Security, also known as the Securitate, was set up.

All banks and large businesses were nationalised, and land was completely removed from private ownership as Gheorghiu-Dej instigated the start of a widescale programme of collectivisation of farms that slowly and brutally began to change the face of the nation.

Following his death in 1965 Gheorghiu-Dej was succeeded by Nicolae Ceausescu, who remained in power until he was deposed by the revolution of December 1989.

That is a very short version of some of the key events which created the world my father grew up in, at a time when his large family lived in a small, two-bedroomed wooden house in Izvoarele Sucevei. But I hope it helps to give context to the environment of fear and lack of security that existed during that era.

The politics and decisions of the communist elite had such a profound and devastating impact on him. The long-term effects spilled out through the post-war generations and extended into the diaspora that would cover so many countries around the world.

In 2020, I returned home and made a short film of my own for YouTube about the building and village where dad had lived. I still find it almost beyond belief that 11 people lived together in that tiny home during the post-war years.

I thought I had a childhood that suffered from a lack of privacy, but I now realise that mine was almost luxurious compared to the conditions of my dad's family and their neighbours after the war. Theirs was a life of extreme poverty. Their only real aims were survival, and to be able to feed and clothe their children in the hope that they might go on to have a better life.

It is very sad that so many millions of young Romanians have left their home country in recent years. But at least we have been able to fulfil some of the hopes and ambitions that were denied to our grandparents, and are now increasingly in a position to help with further economic, social and political developments at home.

It is hard to think of a greater contrast to life in England during the 1950s and 1960s, and the freeform way that British society grew and progressed in those years – whether in music, writing, art, fashion and travel or manufacturing, consumerism, sport and human rights.

Izvoarele Sucevei is still a very small commune in Suceava County in the north of Romania, the equivalent of a rural English village, with a population that rarely goes much above 2,500. It is so small that even when you Google the name today, very little comes up other than the fact that it is rich in deer, bears and wolves, and thus has always been a popular hunting area.

Bordering Ukraine, the commune sits alongside the Suceava River. In the three-hundred years it has existed, it has come under the control of multiple different rulers, which makes it difficult for the people to have a specific sense of their own identity outside of their immediate boundaries.

My father's father worked in the local forest, at a time when they used the water to transport the trunks down the mountains manually. It was a process that now looks to have been slow, but very ecologically sound – especially when compared to the intense and impersonal mechanisation that exists today. Once again, we are able to get a glimpse of their way of work and life on YouTube, as there is a short film from the 1960s that shows the men in action.

After cutting down and stripping the trees, they used horses to drag the trunks to the banks of the Suceava River, where they tethered them together to create giant wooden rafts.

Dams were then created to lift the water levels before everything was all released in one go – thereby using the power of nature to push the wood many miles downstream.

It was very cheap and efficient, but required the men to be strong and work extremely long hours in what could often be a dangerous and unpredictable environment.

There was no safety equipment, and it is astounding to see how the men stood so casually on maybe twenty tethered logs. They wore baggy brown trousers, cotton shirts with rolled-up sleeves, flat caps and leather boots. Invariably, they had a cigarette balanced in the corner of their mouths.

Long pike poles were used to steer the rafts as they were launched down the river at high speed. Water washed across them in great waves as they bounced off the sides, sped down through the forests and mountains, emerged from foaming rapids, and tried to avoid being hit by old or loose logs, which behaved as randomly as riderless horses who have shed their jockeys in the Grand National.

When the rafts reached their destination, and began to slow and drift at the bottom of the river, we saw other workers run along the banks like an excited supporting crowd before dragging them out of the water and loading the sodden logs onto trailers that were then attached to tractors and rapidly driven away.

The old loggers – the fathers and sons and sometimes even grandfathers – were an integral part of their local communities. They understood the trees, and the power of nature and timber seemed to be in their bones. That was what my grandfather did on every working day. While there must have been an incredible sense of teamwork and camaraderie, it cannot have left much time for family life or any other interests.

It must have also been almost impossible for him to feed and clothe such a large family on the very low wages that were coming into the home from this work. Poverty may have been the reason behind my dad's parents making a decision that seems inexplicably cruel and heartless to me, but must have been far more commonplace during that era.

When my dad was only nine or ten years old, he was forced to make a change to his life that I am sure had a shocking and deep impact on his personality. It clearly influenced the man he became, and at least partly explains why he struggled to connect emotionally with his own children.

The details are sketchy, but we do know that one day he was abruptly taken out of school. He was told that he was immediately leaving home and being sent to work on the lands of a rich man and his family. Dad very rarely spoke about it.

Here was an experience so traumatic and upsetting that he tried to permanently bury the memory deep within his soul. But I do remember him once telling me that the family owned a lot of land with many sheep and cows. He was basically used as a child servant.

I assume that they must have been linked to the local communist hierarchy, but it is almost impossible to fully appreciate how awful it would have been for a small boy of that age to be exploited so terribly. This was an exceptionally tough few years for him, during which he received very little education and no love or affection.

It is easy to imagine that he would have withdrawn almost completely into himself as a means of self-preservation, especially as he told me he was expected to do anything the family demanded of him at any time. He was provided with food and shelter but that was pretty much it. His clothes were thin and basic, but the main memory that stuck with him all his life was that he had no shoes to wear, and had to spend his days working and living barefoot.

One of the young Ilie's regular jobs was to be sent into the fields to look after lambs. When the rains came, he would become so immersed in cold mud that the bare skin on his legs and feet would break and blister. The experience left him full of such pain and trauma that he could instantly recall it decades later.

Tragically, he had no-one to care for or look after him. As I look at my own children, I simply cannot envisage how anyone could allow their own boy to be taken from them and put into what was little more than modern slavery. But Ilie was simply left alone to fend for himself.

In writing this book, I have wondered whether he was treated so badly by the people who were effectively his 'owners' because he had a Ukrainian surname. And also if he was sent away by his own parents because he was not a natural child of his father, and could have been a constant reminder of the alleged shame of his mother's experience during war.

I will never know for certain if it was easier for them to have him out of sight, but my dad must have felt completely abandoned, rejected and alone in the world. I don't have much other information, just the occasional snippets from him on the very rare occasions when he would speak about it, but there is no doubt that he was severely traumatised. The whole experience – which lasted several years – was brutalising.

It wasn't until he went into the army in his late teens that he had an opportunity to educate himself, and learn how to relate to other people. Under communism, it was compulsory for young men to be called up. Once he was there, he became obsessed with learning and reading as much as he could, so he could study and pass the exams required for a job as a forester.

He told me that when everyone else was sleeping, he would study at night with a candle. He would strive to concentrate and read so he could complete his lessons, as he was so busy working in the forest during the day.

Perhaps that is where I get my own obsession with work from, and it also helps explain something he was always telling us when we were growing up: that we must go to school, study and graduate, and not go through the kind of miseries he experienced as a boy.

In many ways it was astonishing that he graduated and found the mental strength to survive the pain and rejection of his childhood. He then worked his way up through the forestry hierarchy at a time when he appears to have been a solitary character.

This was in the era when everyone was allocated a job by the government as soon as they finished studying – although in theory they could say if they wanted to work in a particular sector, such as agriculture or engineering.

After the army, he went to West-Central Romania and the small town of Hunedoara in Transylvania. Although he must have spent almost 20 years there, I know very little about his life in this period, other than that he finished his studies and worked in the local forest.

Those two decades are almost complete blanks as far as his children are concerned, and he rarely mentioned them. But one thing that Ilie always retained was a sense of loyalty and attachment to his home village, despite having been forcibly wrenched from his home and childhood.

Although he lived more than 400km from Izvoarele Sucevei, he never forgot that was where his roots lay. Each summer, he ensured that he recruited seasonal workers from both there and the other villages in the Bukovina region to travel to work alongside him in the forests and fields around Hunedoara.

He knew they came from a very poor area, and wanted to provide them with an opportunity to earn money and feed their families. As a large workforce was always required to carry out the many jobs that needed to be done in the forest, it was an arrangement that worked well for everyone.

After almost two decades of relative solitude, his life changed forever in 1981. A group of noisy schoolgirls from the village of Cârlibaba – which sits a few miles south of Izvoarele Sucevei – were among that summer's new recruits.

They included 16-year-old Maria Tironeac and her friends. These young women had decided to travel across Romania to Petrosani, a town close to Hunedoara. They thought they would combine the experience of a three-month working holiday with a break from their home and families, as well as earning themselves some money for new clothes.

Ilie was 37 when he noticed that Maria seemed to stand out from the rest as being strong-willed and unusually mature for her age. They began spending time together away from work. Then, in what is usually described as a 'whirlwind romance,' they fell in love and both their lives promptly turned upside down.

It cannot have been easy for Maria to tell her unsuspecting parents that she was dropping out of school to stay with a man she had just met and barely knew, especially as he was 21 years older than her. They were utterly shocked and devastated, as she was their only child, and they begged her to return home and reconsider.

But having found instant happiness with an experienced and good-looking older man, Maria was stubbornly determined that nothing would change her mind. Just three months after they first met, the pair married on June 5, 1981. Despite strong initial disapproval from family and friends and many turbulent and difficult times, they remained together for 39 years.

Maria had been born on September 6, 1964 to Ilie and Eudochia. Not entirely surprisingly, they strongly disapproved of both my father and the marriage. Relations between them all didn't exactly improve when my sister Ana Maria was born on April 23, 1982. I arrived the following year on August 23. The many hopes and plans they'd had for their daughter didn't include her gaining a husband and two children while she was still in her teens.

Unfortunately – and perhaps inevitably – there were strains in the marriage almost immediately. It was soon after she became pregnant with me that mum decided she'd had enough of all the problems, and that it was time for a return to her home village and the support of her parents.

Having told my dad rather bluntly that she wasn't bothered whether he joined her or stayed where he was, she and Ana Maria travelled north to Cârlibaba. After settling in with her own mum and dad, Maria gave birth to me in the main hospital of the nearby town of Vatra Dornei.

A few weeks passed before my father decided to follow and finally meet his new son. Having closed down his old life and returned to the Suceava region, he did so on the strict condition that his wife and children once again packed their bags as well, and all went to live with him in his own home village of Izvoarele Sucevei.

He knew he would not be welcome at his in-laws, and never really did get on very well with my mother's father. The feeling was entirely mutual. Although my grandparents partly accepted him towards the end of their lives, they were never fully convinced by him.

We all stayed together in the new home for the next six years, with dad working long hours in the forests while mum looked after a young family that never seemed to stop growing – an increasing problem in the very small house we lived in.

My younger sister Stefania Teodora was born on September 24, 1984. Having had three babies in as many years, they took a short break before Ilie arrived on April 17, 1987. My youngest brother Vasilie completed the line up on October 12, 1988.

Unfortunately, my mum wasn't enjoying life in the village as she didn't get on with my father's mother who lived close by. She had very few friends, not least because looking after five small children was such a full-time role. When I was just six years old, she made the huge decision to move home once again and take all of us with her.

This was in August or September 1989, just a few weeks before the revolution that would topple President Ceausescu and lead to the execution of him and his wife on Christmas Day. As young children, though, the only issues we knew about were those of an unhappy home.

There had been problems in their marriage for a long time. My mum had wanted to leave before, but was always prevented by my father who was determined not to let her escape again. This time, she planned everything in secret as though it was a military operation, and waited for an opportunity when she knew he'd be away working in the forest for a few days.

I can remember so clearly the morning we left that home for the last time, as it was warm and sunny. It felt like an exciting day, liberating us from a house that had been a source of so much anxiety and unhappiness.

Mum had prepared all the luggage, and then called us together like a small tribe to explain that we were moving to live with our other grandparents – even though our dad didn't want us to and wasn't going to come with us. But we were going anyway and not to worry as she would take care of us all.

Looking back at the way she arranged to leave him for a second time, I'm just overwhelmed with admiration at the courage and determination that must have taken, especially with five small children and their belongings. Not to mention the sheer organisation involved. At this stage, she was only a young woman of 26 herself. She has truly been an astonishing mum, and I hope she knows how much we all appreciate everything she has done for us throughout our lives.

I still went to school that morning. Even though I didn't understand fully what was going on, I was so excited about having an adventure, and going on a journey. I was also happy that I wouldn't be going back to that particular school as it was very small. I had a feeling of freedom that I was going to escape from that unhappy black hole and go back to Cârlibaba – to a more advanced school that had more kids and was part of a far bigger and more vibrant community.

After school ended in the early afternoon, we all met up together with our bags and walked to the bus stop. It was about 80km to Cârlibaba and took around two hours to get there. But for our little gang, it was like travelling to the other side of the world. It seemed so far away, and you have to remember that in communist Romania we rarely ever went anywhere.

Mum's father, our grandad, was waiting at the bus stop with his horse and cart to take his daughter, five grandchildren and masses of bags and suitcases back to their small home. Here is another example of how far behind the rest of Europe Romania was. Elsewhere that year, Porsche were launching their new 964, but we still relied on real horsepower. Anyone who had a car back then would have been regarded as the king of the village.

Grandad took us home, and said that if our dad wanted

to also come and live with us then he'd be very welcome, but otherwise he and our granny would look after us. I'm sure a part of him would have been very happy for the situation to remain like that, but he was also playing his own mind games with the split to see what my father's next move would be.

For us as a family, it was to be our final major move. Cârlibaba became my main home for most of the next decade. I still love the village, and feel a sense of escape and freedom when I go back there. It's where my Romanian soul feels most connected with the land and people, and that will never change – not least because mum is still living there.

In fact, my dad must have followed us very soon afterwards, as I know he was already in Cârlibaba by the time of the revolution. I remember he'd watch the events on TV and ask us to stay quiet while he tried to hear what was going on and work out what it might mean for him and our family.

He spoke to his bosses and managed to move his forestry job to Cârlibaba, while we were also given a house by the local government association. That sounds very generous, but it was just a small one-bedroom home for the seven of us to live in.

It was tough, and must have been exceptionally difficult yet again for my mum as she tried to look after all of us with no space, a low income, and seven mouths to feed. But, as ever, she somehow managed to make it all work.

The cooking, eating and sleeping all had to take place in those two rooms. As we didn't even have a bathroom, we had to go outside to use the toilet, which was not a happy experience in the very cold winter months we endured during that time.

But with dad working in the forest as one of the rangers, and mum obtaining a part-time cleaning job in the building where the local district forestry organisation was based, we just about had enough income.

A couple of years later, we managed to get allocated a three-bedroom house with a loft that had become available on the opposite side of the road. It was rent-free as it was provided by dad's employer. That seemed almost like a palace to us when we first arrived, but it never felt like a particularly warm or friendly place that we could relax in as our home.

I don't think my parents ever really had a happy marriage as everything moved so fast in their early years that they didn't get an opportunity to spend time together. Those were the lost years when, in a parallel universe, they might have been able to grow and develop and get to know each other properly.

My mum was married only three months after meeting my dad, with her first child being born when she was only 17 – still not much more than a kid herself. She definitely missed out on her teenage years.

They had many arguments, verbal and physical, and when I was a small child my mum had to run from the house on a number of occasions as she was scared about what might happen if she stayed in the same room with him.

But she always returned later the same day, as she knew she had a responsibility to look after her children. Despite all their problems, and the way he often treated her, she still genuinely loved him.

Because of the size of the house, there was literally no hiding place at home. My siblings and I heard and witnessed many of the fights, which I found very traumatic and frightening. I'm sure they were a big contributor to the problems dad and I had throughout our lives.

As an adult, I can now appreciate how difficult it is to be a child who is torn between wanting the love and guidance of a father, while at the same time being afraid of him and in an almost permanent state of anxiety.

Even though I loved him, it hasn't always been easy to forgive and often difficult to forget. My parents were on the edge of divorce several times. On reflection, maybe it would have been better for both of them if they had gone through with it.

Part of the problem was that dad didn't have many friends. There was no-one for him to share his thoughts and worries with. As I said earlier, he was a very cold and distant man who sometimes seemed crazy and had no interest in socialising. I realise now that all this can almost certainly be traced back to the isolation and loss of his childhood.

Although he encouraged us to study, we never had books in the house as there was neither the money nor time for them. Until his final years and period of ill health, he had no religious beliefs. When I was growing up, he spent almost his whole time working, and rarely went to church unless it was to celebrate a special occasion or a festival.

Dad was a member of the communist party, because in those days everyone had to be registered if they wanted to keep their job. But I don't think he really had any strong political views, because his focus was always on practical things and survival. He never seemed to be at all interested in events that took place outside Romania.

How many times did he leave the country? There was a visit to Israel, and one to London when I got married, plus a holiday in Greece with my family. That was it. There were certainly never any holidays when I was as child, nor did he show curiosity about other countries, or the world outside our immediate orbit.

After he retired at the compulsory state age of 63, my father stayed at home and looked after his cows, pigs, chickens and horses in the rural area where they still lived. It looked as though he had found a degree of peace and calmness, and that he and our mum would finally have many happy years together to rest and spend time with their children and grandchildren. But it wasn't to be.

In 2019, we were all deeply shocked to be told that he had developed cancer in his stomach. From the moment of diagnosis, dad was on borrowed time. Although we took him to many leading hospitals and specialists, and he had chemotherapy and tried several other treatments, there was nothing that could slow the steady spreading of the disease.

I tried to visit my parents as often as my work and family commitments would allow, but dad didn't really mellow with me until those final weeks when we spent time together, slowly walking and talking in the forest.

Even now, I don't feel that I really knew him as a man, or fully understood what was in his head. But I am pleased that it was the first time we had become closer. It was also the first time he ever told me that he loved me.

I had just told him that I was going to stand as an Independent candidate for the Romanian Senate. He looked at me and said *'I don't know why you want to get involved in politics, because you will come across lots of dishonest and unreliable people.'* I told him it is important that good people get involved, and make a difference for the future generations that will follow.

'At the end of the day it is your choice,' he replied. *'But you know what? I love you.'* I replied that I loved him as well, and that was it – the one moment of genuine emotion that he ever displayed to me.

On October 21, 2020, just three days after he died, Ilie's family and friends gathered at my parents' home in Cârlibaba to say farewell as he began his final journey at the base of the mountains he had climbed all his life.

Despite the Covid restrictions, so many people came to pay their respects that we were a little concerned the police might take an interest. But fortunately we were left alone to mourn as we buried him in the local churchyard.

I hope he has finally found some peace. He always kept a roof over our heads, clothes on our backs, and food on the table. I have no doubt that the horrendous childhood exploitation that he experienced – plus the shocking rejection by his parents when he was a young boy – contributed enormously to the cold and difficult man we all knew.

Despite all those problems, I realise now that he motivated me to be stronger and more focused. I wanted to fight – to show him that I was better than he thought, and better than he said. That became important for me to demonstrate, and I am sure it played a role in my determination to set up and grow my own business empire.

After I first moved away, it was a long time before I visited my parents at home. Dad used to tell me, with predictable regularity, that if I didn't listen to what he said and follow his steps then I would be a loser. I constantly had to tell him – and remind myself – that no, that was not how my life was going to be. And that, far from being a loser, I'd show him how good I was.

He was always telling me to work hard. He emphasised how important it was to spend time in school, gaining knowledge that would help me look after my own children and family and succeed in my own life.

But, in those days, life for most Romanians was like a machine set up to contain and control the people. With very few opportunities for individuals or businesses to be creative and flourish, that didn't excite me.

Now that I am a father myself, I feel I have a much better and more enlightened understanding of what he must have meant. But I also realise that, because of his own childhood traumas, he didn't know how to be a good father for the simple reason that no one had really cared for him as a child. Ultimately, I am the son of my father, but I am not my father's son.

4

Growing Up

In the absence of a real relationship with my father, it was my grandfather – my mother's father – who became the most important influence on me when I was growing up. The complete opposite to my dad in almost every way, he was a very organised and calm man who wouldn't do anything to hurt anyone.

Fortunately, my grandparents were also near to Cârlibaba, living only about 4km from us. As they had spare bedrooms, I would often spend several weeks at a time with them during my teenage years. I enjoyed the chance to have some space of my own, and get away from the arguments and stress.

Like most men in the region, grandad worked in the forest helping to maintain the woods and paths, while sometimes assisting the local people with their cows. He was a hard worker, and I had a lot of time for him.

I remember one summer during the early 1990s when one of his horses became pregnant, and he gave me the foal when it was born. It was one of the most amazing days of my life when he woke me up on a warm and sunny morning and asked me to go with him as he had a special present waiting for me.

We walked to the barn, and there was this beautiful small foal. He was pure white, like his mum, and I was awestruck as I watched him struggling to stay upright on his spindly legs, learning to balance, and getting milk from his mother. It was one of the happiest occasions of my childhood, and the first time I'd ever actually owned something myself.

At first, I didn't believe him. It seemed beyond possibility that someone would give me such an extraordinary gift. But once I accepted that, yes, the horse really was mine to keep, I called him Puiu – which means baby in English.

He lived with my grandparents, but as I was with them so often during that period, I was able to spend many hours feeding and grooming him, and eventually riding him bareback in the hills and forests.

As I grew older, and was spending increasingly long periods away from home at school and then overseas, I let my dad use him, and he lived as a working horse for almost 25 years. His life ended in a terrible way, when my father tied him up one evening on a slope while it was raining.

As the horse was getting very old and unsteady, it was a foolish thing to do. Tragically, Puiu slipped in the mud, and was strangled by the rope. It was dreadful, but rather than apologise and acknowledge what he had done, my dad cried and complained that he no longer had a horse. Nor did I.

My grandfather was, quite simply, one of the best men I have ever met. He was very well respected by everyone in the village – a good man to be around with great energy and a nice vibe. I'd go to his house and notice that all his tools were in their correct place, and that every fence was straight.

After the heavy winter snow in Cârlibaba, the fences would sometimes move, and because they had maybe three or four acres of land around the house for their animals to live on, it was very important to put them back in place at the start of each spring. He always made sure that everything was repaired, painted and tidied up. I would love the whole environment. In contrast, my dad never had straight fences.

My granny was also immensely important. She was the one person able to help me emotionally when I was a teenager. She would support me in front of my dad when he was shouting at me. She'd tell him that he needed to trust his son. She would try to help him understand that I wanted to experiment with new things, and encourage him to give me the freedom to do something different with my life.

Naturally, my dad would completely disagree. He would shout that I needed to listen to him, and do everything as he said or things wouldn't be ok. It was as though he wanted me to be chained to him, and never to disobey his wishes, because he'd already planned out my life and career. He simply expected me to take over his forest job when he retired. It was like a mantra.

Granny played a huge role in giving me confidence and we had a deep mutual trust. She was literally the shoulder I cried on when I didn't understand why my dad was so rude, and wouldn't keep his promises to me. She was a lovely lady – gentle and wise and encouraging.

She would tell me not to worry, as I would have plenty of time to do my own thing in the future when I grew up and had my own family and success. She would often cook for me, and always protected and helped and supported me. Both of my grandparents were great for me, and together they had a very positive impact on my life.

I realise that I haven't yet spoken much about my mother, but I have always had a much better and less complicated relationship with her. She was always there for us, but had an extremely difficult life and many issues to deal with.

To be living with a difficult and unpredictable man who was two decades older than her and spent long hours away in the forest, while bringing up a demanding family in a tiny house with very little money amid all the other stresses of the Ceausescu and post-revolutionary period, must have felt impossible at times. I have huge admiration for how she coped and survived.

Looking back, I can see that her life was one continuous and repetitive daily routine of cooking, cleaning, washing, shopping, queuing and arguments. I cannot imagine doing that myself, and I don't know how she found time to be herself – to be Maria.

Thank goodness her parents lived close by, and were able to support her and our family and be a safe space.

Still, despite all the problems, she was our mum. She looked after us, and was the one who shared the love.

In many ways, Bukovina was a wonderful place to grow up. We were surrounded by woods and hills and rivers and, of course, animals. When we were very young, we didn't imagine there could be anywhere more beautiful in the world.

I also liked the mix of nationalities. We had Romanians, Ukrainians, Germans, Hungarians and Poles all living there. The local language was a strange hybrid that incorporated many different words.

The Ukrainian of my region, for example, has amalgamated so many Romanian words that a visitor from Kiev would probably find it quite difficult to understand. Fortunately, I have always found it very easy to learn new languages. As well as Romanian and Ukrainian, I can now also speak English, Portuguese and some French.

To have so many different traditions around me was a good experience. I learned a lot from all these diverse cultures, while also becoming very comfortable with all the different voices and accents. That was particularly valuable in later life when I moved to London. You can easily encounter 30 different nationalities when you step into a single carriage on the London Underground!

There were other benefits as well, especially when it came to food and presents. My dad was born in a region where they follow the Russian tradition of celebrating Christmas on January 6, but we also used to have our normal Christmas on December 25. We'd have our first celebration at home and then enjoy a second one at my dad's parents' house a few days later.

That was also the closest we ever got to a family holiday. Other than those Christmas trips, I don't remember that we ever went away for a genuine break. It would have been lovely to have visited the Black Sea coastline as a child, but we simply didn't have the money, and my first glimpse of the sea didn't come until much later when I moved to Portugal.

There is so much about Romania that the rest of the world seems to be unaware of, including the large network of spa resorts across the country. Unfortunately, many of them have been to left to collapse in recent years because of underinvestment, but my dad used to occasionally visit them during the Ceausescu era.

State employees were given tickets to go to the thermo spars at the Black Sea or Oradea, where the hot mineral water comes up from underground. I remember when he went for a couple of weeks with my mum and I stayed with my grandparents. It was a good break for him, and he came back a different person. Unfortunately, that didn't last long, and he was soon back to normal.

By 1990, life had become a little more modern than that portrayed in the Radu film, but not by much as we were still very backward compared to most of Europe at that time.

There were maybe 2500 people living in Cârlibaba, and although it some ways it felt safe and was a very friendly place, it was also anxious and insular with very little privacy. Everyone knew your business.

Cârlibaba was, and still is, a mainly one-road village. The DN18 winds through the valley, alongside the river that gave the place its name. Dense forest covered hills and mountains on either side. Clusters of small white houses were dotted around the smaller side roads, often with horses, sheep and cows in the meadows.

With their red and brown roofs, narrow slit windows and piles of logs outside, it looked as though the place had hardly been touched by the modern world. Now, of course, anyone can log onto Google World and take a virtual drive around the whole area!

As I mentioned earlier, our home was very small and only had two main rooms for the seven of us to live in. It was a semi-detached house on a side street. We had a little garden at the front, and a field at the back where we kept our cows, chickens, pigs and a horse.

That is not something I've ever seen in Wembley, where I've lived for the past decade. But it was completely normal in the village, as we needed the animals' produce to feed the family and pay the relentless, punitive Government taxes. It was quite a long garden, maybe as much as 150m, but we'd still be breathing in the smell of the cows and pigs when the wind was blowing towards us.

Step inside my front door. You'll see a corridor that led to the small bathroom, then another one leading to a room at the front where my dad used to keep his guns and tools. Then some steps to the loft, which was never fully finished and primarily used for storage. Our main room served simultaneously as a kitchen, dining room, living room and bedroom.

It had a massive fireplace, a table, some storage units and a sofa where our parents slept. Eventually, we bought a fridge and a washing machine, probably in 1993 or 1994. But we had few of the appliances that we all now take for granted.

Before then, mum had spent a lot of time each week hand-washing the seemingly never–ending piles of our clothes. Eventually, they were able to purchase a small twin tub with a belt. There was no dryer so she used a mangle and hung the clothes out to dry in the back field when the weather was warm, or indoors by the fire during the cold and miserable winter months.

We did have electricity, but there was no central heating, so the fireplaces in each room were essential to keep us alive. At least we lived next to a forest so there was never a shortage of fuel, which was just as well as the cooker was a wood-burning one.

I can still clearly recall how mum would use the dried logs to start a fire as soon as she woke up, so that we'd be able to have a first coffee about 15 minutes later. When I was about 12, we had a gas fire installed and were thrilled that it seemed to be so luxurious. But we always kept a close eye on the gas, which was stored outside in canisters and needed guarding from passing travellers.

Our only bedroom was shared by all five of us children, which meant no privacy. To fit us all in, we had bunk beds. Being the eldest boy, I was at least always on the top. But my brother kept falling onto the floor, so dad eventually replaced it with a bigger bed that we shared, while making the room even more cramped.

We had to get on with it as that was all we knew, but it was more like a dormitory than a bedroom. It became just a place to sleep in, rather than one that we could ever escape into for teenage solitude. I certainly couldn't try to personalise it by putting posters up, because my sisters wouldn't have liked to be surrounded by footballers.

But we had a playing corner outside by the woodstore, and that was where I kept my stuff. It was my only chance at privacy. There was nowhere else for me to sit on my own and, anyway, I didn't have many possessions that were exclusively mine.

We had an outside toilet, which I hated, and also a special warm-water tank that served as a makeshift shower. We would fill the drum with water, and then rush to hurriedly get underneath and clean ourselves as best as we could before it quickly ran out.

As I mentioned earlier, to get away from this cramped environment I increasingly went to stay with my grandparents, who had a much bigger house. I was able to actually have my own room when I visited them, which was a huge thrill, so I would try and live there for many weeks at a time from when I was about nine or ten.

Unlike in our home, my grandparents had some books and music, and even an old– fashioned record-player with an arm. I loved lowering it when the records were dusty and hearing the strange whirring noises.

However, even my grandfather could be a little wayward at times, particularly if we went to the pub with his friends after work. He would drink beer, sometimes cognac, and often a weird thing that I think was like a form of vodka made out of prunes. Once they got talking and drinking, it was a challenge to get him home.

Granny would tell me that I had to make sure I brought him back with me. But I was only a child, and very easily bribed by a packet of sweets or a soft drink. I'd sit on my own next to them, or under the table. Grandad would have one shot, and then another, followed by a couple more.

Suddenly it was 10pm and he'd be comfortably drunk.

By the time I finally managed to get through to his conscience by whining that I was tired and wanted to get to bed, I had usually failed hopelessly in my mission, and would then have to avoid granny catching my ears as she demanded to know why we'd been so long. When I ran into my room, I used to shout back that she should ask him as I was just a kid and he didn't take any notice of me.

It is interesting to recall that, at that time, it was always men who were in the pubs. I don't remember ever seeing women drinking before the 1990s, but after the revolution they opened the pubs and cafés, and you'd suddenly see women sitting down and socialising with their friends as well.

The pubs were nothing like the ones today, being very basic rooms with poor décor: a few tables and chairs and perhaps some bookshelves. They were for drinking and talking and not a lot more. The Western European concept of the gastro-pub was still galaxies away from the northern outreaches of Romania.

Looking back, I realise that I became detached from my family home from an early age. That helped me become more independent, as I was happiest doing things alone. This mindset has certainly contributed to my more recent successes. When you are running a company, decision-making and leadership can be a solitary business.

During that period, Ana Maria spent a lot of time with our grandparents as well. She was definitely the 'big sister', and not just because she was the eldest. It was an integral part of her identity. She was very tough, and when she was in charge she would make us clean the house and only have one slice of bread to eat.

She spent a lot of her childhood with granny and grandad because she had some problems as a baby, when she was diagnosed as anaemic and subsequently needed a lot of medication. Granny was only 43 when Ana Maria was born in 1982, so for her it was like having another child – not least because they had only had my mum themselves.

Because of where we grew up, and the lack of indoor space, ours was very much an outdoor childhood. I didn't have many friends apart from my family, largely because everyone was so suspicious of each other during that era, and I mainly played with my brothers and sisters.

There were a few boys that I played football with, but that was about all. There was very little traffic, and the school was almost next door to our home, so it seemed to be a very safe environment.

I was always an active person, and learned to ride when I was a small child. Grandad would sit me on a horse when he was working in the forest. He'd be taking the logs out for transport, and let me go with him and see what he was doing.

Even when I wasn't staying at his house, I'd run down there early in the morning just so I could ride the horse as he went to work. He would put me on its back, pick up the food my granny had prepared, and we'd go together into the forest.

As I was so young, I'd get tired easily and usually fall asleep mid-morning, which must have been a relief to him as it gave him a break from the constant questions I apparently bombarded him with.

After that, we'd have lunch, and I enjoyed spending the afternoon with the horse, although the affection wasn't always returned. I was so small that he'd often pull his head round and throw me into the bushes! Fortunately, I was already developing my determined and stubborn side and wouldn't give up.

At other times I'd be with my siblings. We'd look for a nest where we could take some eggs, and then hide them in each other's hair before slapping it. I'm not sure I'd approve of that now, or let my kids disturb the nests, but at that time it seemed natural fun and we just didn't want to be indoors. We'd run and play or fish until we heard our mum calling for us to come in. But that often wasn't until 10 or 11pm.

We each had our daily chores, such as bringing wood inside for the fire, looking after the horse, or feeding the chickens and pigs. I hated doing them, but I had no choice as my sister would have reported me to my dad, and I knew I'd get punished.

I had to put in the hours, but I was never a happy or willing worker – which is ironic as I ended up becoming a workaholic when I moved to London and started my own company. I guess that neatly sums up the difference between communism and capitalism.

We only had a small black-and-white television that was mainly used for watching sport and cartoons, and sometimes the news. I think there were just a couple of state-owned TV stations, and they pumped out relentless propaganda so there were few reasons to stay indoors. It also had a lot of transmission problems, and the picture used to come and go on a regular basis, which didn't do a lot for my dad's temper.

A decade after the revolution, there was one particular entertainment programme I will never forget, and which began on Romanian TV in 1999. It was called *Surprise, Surprise*, and was a very emotional show as they'd reunite long lost relatives and friends and give them a massive surprise in the studio.

I remember how we all used to wait for the programme to come on. I was fascinated to see shots of the audience in the studio, and the big reveal when a long-lost or unknown uncle or cousin would appear from the side of the set to shock the family on the sofa.

Then they would all burst into tears. It was probably the only show we'd ever watch together as a family at home. I was always hoping that one day we'd be invited on, and meet a relative we'd forgotten about, before discovering that they were a multi-millionaire or a striker with Steaua Bucharest!

The TV was our only technology, as we didn't have a computer at home and mobiles were still a thing of the future. I think I was probably about 17 when I got my first phone and it was a Nokia that looked like a brick and was half the size of my head.

Unsurprisingly, it wasn't easy to get a strong enough signal to actually make a call in those days. It wasn't really until I was in Portugal that I became familiar with the internet, and discovered how to use Messenger and Yahoo to stay in touch with people.

Now, of course, it is very different in Cârlibaba. The houses have broadband and fibreoptics and multi-channel TV, and everyone seems to be on Facebook, Instagram and TikTok. But I sometimes wonder if perhaps, amid the many benefits that connectivity has brought to the community, they haven't also lost something special. Life seems to have moved from people engaging with the forests and rivers to just taking and posting photos of them.

When I was young, I walked a lot with my dad, and I remember the elation and thrill of seeing bears in the wild when he took me up into the mountains. One Sunday we stood silently as we watched a mum with her two cubs eating raspberries just 60 or 70 metres away.

At times like that, I felt completely safe, as he always took his hunting gun with him. But we were often warned about the wolves and bears in the countryside. I used to hear wolves howling in the night and it was sometimes very scary.

We were told that, if we ever found ourselves confronted by a wolf when we were on our own, it was extremely important to stand very quiet and still and not run away as then they would leave you alone. Fortunately, I have not yet had to test that advice and find out if it is true.

In my village, there were a few local cafés and restaurants, but it wasn't really until the mid-1990s that some other options began to appear. A few local entrepreneurs felt confident enough to invest in new businesses, and I seem to remember that we even had a disco bar with lights, which was a bit like Vegas coming to Cârlibaba.

Throughout the Ceausescu era, the shops were state-run co-operatives, and the only place where people could buy all their food such as meat, bread, oil and sugar. But the options were very limited, so people would try and supplement it with vegetables grown on their own small allotments, and by keeping some livestock.

The problem was that everyone was required to hand

their produce over to the state, and it was forbidden to keep any lambs and pigs for yourself and your family. All animals were registered with the local vet, and when they were fully grown they had to be transported to a state market, where a small fee was paid and the animals were taken away.

State officials would come to collect the produce from each village every month, and then export them abroad to help pay off the enormous debts Ceausescu had run up in the 1970s. I remember how my grandad would nurture and grow a massive bull, perhaps to 500 or 600 kilos, but he would have to give it to the government. Even at that age, I knew it was very unfair.

I've also got no doubt that a number of local communist officials will have eaten extremely well after the monthly collections. This was the reality of how our communism actually worked, because favouritism, nepotism and corruption were the norm.

Sadly, very little changed after the revolution, as food subsidies were cut, prices increased and inflation came close to 260 per cent in 1993, which was devastating for the vast majority who were on subsistence or low wages.

The villagers had little option but to try to cheat the system and find a way to keep something back to feed their families. The penalties were high, but sometimes a piglet would be hidden and kept secret as soon as it was born, rather than being declared to the vet.

There were very few fridges and no freezers, so the animal would be furtively fed and fattened. After slaughter, it would be stored in a drum of salt to preserve it, then hidden underground.

The reason we were all so careful was because of

the Securitate, the state's brutal and feared secret police. It has been estimated that as many as one in four of the population were informers of some kind.

That created an ever-present atmosphere of paranoia, fear and distrust, and was one of the reasons people tended to stick with their family groups – because to bring an outsider into a conversation could create a potential risk. The whole nation was cut off from the outside, and we had very little knowledge of what was going on elsewhere. It all added up to a feeling of great oppression.

I was very aware of it, even as a small child, and we were always being warned that we had to be careful about what we said as the adults were afraid of the consequences. It wasn't just that we could never discuss politics, or wonder what was going on outside of Romania, but also that we had to be careful about every single tiny aspect of our lives.

We couldn't tell anyone that we were even eating meat at home, because there were restrictions and people might get jealous or suspicious and report us. If my grandad killed and hid a pig, we had to stay silent. That was the degree of sickness there was in that time, especially for the poor.

Many of those people who created that fear are still involved in running the country now. They succeeded in completely escaping any kind of justice, by calmly changing their job titles and uniforms, and presenting a reinvented 'democratic' face to the world following the execution of Ceausescu and his wife.

It was a dark era in our history, when everything in our lives was controlled by other people, but tragically even today little has really changed, especially in areas such as national and local government agencies.

There is so much ingrained bureaucracy, relentless red-tape and a shameful lack of accountability that has resulted in much of the country still being stuck in a mindset of corruption and poverty. Unless someone fresh comes in and takes control, it is hard to see how it is going to change.

It was only really when I grew older, and travelled around Europe, that I came to realise the enormous and subliminal impact that the Romanian culture of the 1980s and 90s must have had on me. I always find it very difficult to trust people, and I still have a natural inclination to work with family members and friends and others from my region.

That is slowly changing, but I didn't really feel a difference and a lifting of that fear until I got my British citizenship. Only then was I part of a different family. On that day in 2016, I was so proud.

I felt very conscious that everything had changed, and that I had been adopted by Britain. It was a strongly spiritual experience, as I believed I would now be ok. It took much of that lifelong hidden anxiety away.

But that was still all a long way in the future when I went on my own into the village for the very first time. I was five or six years old, and it was the biggest trip of my young life as I was trusted with buying some bread. I was facing the world, and I felt as though I was now a grown up.

It was only a tiny village, of course, but I was paying attention to everything: the people, the trees, the buildings and the occasional traffic. I clearly remember going into the bakery and giving the baker my family name as I reached up to hand him my money.

In return, he solemnly handed me my allocation. I proudly took hold of the loaf, and for the first time I experienced the meaning of freedom and responsibility. That soon evaporated, of course, when I took the bread home and gave it to my mum and was immediately ordered out into the field to collect the wood and do my chores!

Even in the early 1990s, all the bread in Romania was allocated and restricted. Until new private bakeries and businesses began to appear in the years following the revolution, everything we needed was produced by a local state-run co-operative.

After the new regime came in, that system – like so much of life in Romania – fell apart as people started to steal and keep as much as they could for their own families. What happened was unbelievable.

There was a limit to what was available in Cârlibaba, so we occasionally had to travel to other shops. Our nearest town of Vatra Dornei was about 40km away, and we took the bus when we wanted to visit.

The communists ensured that the bus timetables were organised to fit working patterns, so the buses used to leave the village at 6am, 8.30am, 12noon, 3pm and 7pm. It was very regular and structured, but this was another system that fell apart after the revolution.

The bureaucracy disintegrated, and it resulted in chaos, with so many struggling rural communities finding themselves cut off.

Set in the Carpathian Mountains, Vatra Dornei is one of Romania's oldest and best-known spa and ski resorts.

But in common with other parts of the country, it has seen a steady drain of young people in recent years.

I am convinced it has huge potential to be a wonderful asset for Bukovina and the wider region if it could attract imaginative and ambitious investors. I'd like to see someone come in to develop the resort in a sympathetic way for the local environment, while simultaneously creating jobs and wealth for the community.

Every couple of weeks, our mum would go there to do her main shop and come back with some large bags of food. If we were lucky, there would be some treats as well. We also occasionally bought our clothes there, but the options were always very limited as we had so little money.

Everything had to have a practical purpose and be long lasting. As we were poor, the clothes got passed down. I was very fortunate to be the eldest boy as I usually got things when they were new, unlike poor Ilie and Vasilie.

By contrast, I remember the very happy shock when I first went to Portugal and discovered that I could buy oranges or bananas. In fact, I could buy whatever I wanted, whenever I wanted it. For a young man from a backward Romanian village, it was simply mind blowing to discover what was always available in the shops in the rest of Europe. Obviously, after 1989 a few more things were obtainable, but we were such a low-income family that we couldn't afford them regularly.

During the summer, and from a young age, I recall how Ana Maria and I would try to make extra shopping money by collecting and selling the wild mushrooms that grew in the forest. She was always better than me, as I was a bit lazy, which seems to have been a recurring theme as I look back at my childhood, but we'd save the money. Then, when my mum went to the city, we'd go with her to buy some clothes.

I also remember that the 'big shop' was always in September, just before the new school year began. Dad would take us all to buy new clothes, trainers, books and everything else that we needed. It was amazing.

It felt like a massive holiday for us and it was so exciting when we were allowed to buy new bags. Even if I bought a Bentley now, my happiness wouldn't come close to the excitement I felt back then, as these things were actually mine and were new.

Dad saved for this day for a whole year, and worked hard to clothe us as best as he could. I now realise that sometimes he had to borrow the money, but we probably weren't aware of that at the time.

When things did start to change very slightly after the revolution, the first thing I really remember were the denim jeans coming in from Turkey. Some people must have made a fortune, as the demand for those was so great.

Gradually, some other shops started to appear, and everyone thought the world was about to change dramatically for the better. Unfortunately, that early excitement and optimism was misplaced, and I witnessed the failures in the following years as the country began to steadily collapse.

The mines started to close, and upkeep of the forests fell into a terrible state of chaos. Despite all the very obvious failings and horrors of communism, the Ceausescus had presided over a very organised society where everyone had a job.

Unfortunately, the downside of the revolution was an explosion of bad management and corruption. There was mass theft of assets by the elites as many people rushed to line their own pockets while ignoring the wider population, as well as the need for essential maintenance of the country's infrastructure.

Even as a small child, I noticed the logistics of the area beginning to change in the early 1990s, as the work in the forests was steadily run down. For example, in our region there were something like 30 trucks working in the woods each day. But when they broke down , they were steadily reduced until just five or six remained, and then the business closed.

The same happened on many local farms, and from 1989 to 2000 I witnessed every single stage of failure. The new government took over with the aim of consolidating their own power, but with no plan on how to actually govern. As a direct result, unemployment and inflation dramatically rose, and impacted enormously on the poorest communities in areas such as Bukovina.

In the past, there had always been employment opportunities. Even the small villages had several firms who would look after the forest and the logging and provide local jobs. But the new administration sold out to German and Austrian companies, who had their own agendas, and saw a great opportunity to make a lot of money.

They were given licences to work in the wood and take over the logging and manufacturing, and a way of life that local Romanians had known for many generations was destroyed in a very short time. The result, as we all know, was that millions of us left the country.

The new Romania had the opportunity to keep everyone there and working to build a new and better nation, if the government had only known how to manage the assets, but so much has been sold off and is now foreign-owned. Now they want to sell the airline, the electric network, and the last bank that they own. They will sell everything and end up with nothing.

We had lived in a very restricted society under Ceausescu, and knew great hardship. But after his execution, many from the criminal classes took charge of some areas of government, and vast amounts of money vanished into private accounts. They had no interest in what they undoubtedly viewed as the boring elements of government, but saw an opportunity for themselves.

Across the whole country, the state of the infrastructure is terrifying as railways, roads, utilities and housing crumble. What makes it even more shocking is the fantastic potential that we have in Romania, especially as an untapped tourist destination.

So few people outside our nation seem to know about the mountains, rivers, skiing, beaches and history that is all waiting to be discovered. The incredible painted monasteries should be one of the wonders of the world, as they are so original and beautiful.

I first went to visit one when I was about 14, and we learned how they were built by Stefan the Great when he was ruling Moldavia between 1457 and 1504. He fortified the country, saw off Hungarian, Polish and Ottoman attempts to conquer the region, and was said to have won 34 of his 36 battles.

After each victory, he ordered a new painted monastery or church to be built. As a result, the countryside is dotted with these magnificent places of worship that are unique masterpieces of art and architecture.

We were never really a religious family, and dad paid no attention to church during his working life as he was too busy. But when he got old, like so many people, he started going back to church every Sunday.

My own experience with faith has been mixed. When I was growing up, I had a lot of internal frustration about being poor and the lack of opportunities in life. I couldn't see what the church could offer someone like me.

As I was a loner, I also felt uncomfortable being part of a crowd who all did things together. My mum would often tell me that she thought there was something wrong with me, as I'd rather reject religion and do things my own way.

I remember that I did once agree to go with them to see a priest, but he simply confirmed my prejudices by telling me to have a proper haircut and that I should behave myself like a normal human!

I didn't react well, telling my mum that I had to get away from him otherwise I was likely to punch him, which would not have been the best of reputations for a moody teenager to have.

I think my view on life and spirituality began to change when I first moved to Portugal, and I started to think more about life and humanity and religion. Gradually I felt that we cannot each just be a random mistake, but there must be a bigger process, and we all have something to accomplish.

That thought has grown across the years. I have also

learned that many people believe in different things. I feel that faith is something that should be very personal, and that we need to respect all religions and their followers.

I think there is a power, a karma. If you do good things, you are going to end up in a good place – and this applies to the jobs that you do as well. If you are straight, do quality work, and focus on the community and the environment, success will follow. When you start cutting corners, losing your balance, and not following the rules or caring for other people, then you risk going the other way.

I passionately believe that every action you take has an impact, and if you do good, you get good energy back in return. When I go to an Orthodox church, I find a peace within myself. The liturgy is relaxing and calming to listen to – especially in a modern world where we get so little time for ourselves and are surrounded by the relentless intrusion of technology.

Being in a church must be one of the few places where we are not under the eye of a surveillance camera, just the all-seeing eye of God.

My next awakening came when I was based in Paris, and started going regularly to church, partly because I was alone and it was somewhere I could meet other Romanians. On the second Sunday after I arrived in the city, someone suggested I went to a service with him. But after I set off from my home, I realised I had no clue which station I should get out at, or how to get to the church.

At that point, I was terrified of the Metro as it seemed very complicated and I spoke no French. And yet, for some reason, I experienced a calmness as I just believed I would find it, and that everything would be ok.

Something in my head told me to get out at a random station. When I emerged onto the streets, I started walking along the road – and then suddenly, to my right, I heard church bells pealing.

I looked across, and there was the very church I was seeking. I was astonished. I had no rational explanation for what had happened, and was very surprised, but accepted it. I began to attend regularly. As a direct result of that day, as I'll explain later, I ended up in London and in a position to write this book.

Before I moved abroad, I had only once been on an underground train. It was in circumstances that perfectly sum up the uncertainties we all faced during those immediate years after the revolution.

I cannot recall the exact date, but I know it was in the early 1990s, because after Ceausescu was removed dad was very worried about his job in Cârlibaba. Remember that he was responsible for seven people, and needed an income to look after them all – as well as the animals.

He was aware that, at local level, everyone seemed to be using and abusing their personal relationships to carve up the jobs. Interviews were usually a complete sham. So he made the incredible decision to go to Bucharest and try to speak directly to the minister responsible for the forests.

Dad's two objectives were to confirm his job was safe, and also to try to get my mum some employment. He was aware that some vacancies were coming up locally when a number of older workers were due to retire.

The problem was that Bucharest was well over 500km from our village. Not only did dad make the trip, but he took all five of us children with him to put the maximum possible emotional pressure on the minister.

We must have looked like a brood of ducklings following along behind their parent as we travelled to the capital city. That was the first time I encountered the Bucharest underground, and I was very scared as I had never seen anything like it.

To go on an escalator was an equal mix of terrifying and exciting, as I didn't even realise that staircases could move. Having travelled around the world since that time, I now know that the Romanian metro system is very primitive compared to most others. But, on that day, I was genuinely in a state of awe at these new sights and experiences. I felt as though I had stepped into a movie.

Astonishingly, the Minister agreed to meet us, and was clearly taken by surprise when an entire family trooped into the office. My dad set out his argument: that after working in the forest for many years, and with all these children to feed, it was very unfair that he was being denied the chance to apply for work because of local corruption and nepotism. He was very worried that he might soon be unemployed, which would have had devastating consequences for the whole family.

I suspect the Minister simply wanted rid of us as soon as possible, so he phoned a regional administrator, and insisted that he immediately resolved the situation for my father. Which is exactly what happened.

Maybe a less difficult man would never have dared to take such drastic action, but my dad ensured his job was secure and the emotional pressure undeniably worked. Unfortunately, the local bosses still refused to give my mum a job, probably in revenge for the way my dad went over their heads in such dramatic style.

I was very lucky when I was child, as I didn't have any serious illnesses or injuries, despite always being outside. The main aches and bruises were invariably caused by horses, as I was regularly bitten and hit by them, and often thrown off when trying to ride them bareback.

But I was determined never to give up, and became very single-minded, even though they always seemed to win our battle of wills.

The falls could be painfully hard, leaving me breathless and shocked, but it was my own fault. There were lots of horses in the village, so we'd set them off in the fields and then try to grab them and leap up to see how long we could stay on for.

They would go crazy and buck and leap and shake their heads, until we finally lost our grip and hit the ground. There was never any dignity about the inevitable outcome, but it was a lot of fun, and I learned how to respect and handle these wonderful animals.

From a very young age, I was also very curious, and always wanted to learn practical things. I remember that, when I was developing my reading in my second or third year in school, I found a book about the work of electricians, and became engrossed in the colours and diagrams.

Around that time, I heard my grandmother say she needed a light in one of the storage rooms. As I didn't like the thought of her going outside in the dark, I announced that I could do it for her, and she let me! I must have asked her to buy the cable, but I did all the actual wiring on my own. I ran the cable outside, plugged it into the socket, and was thrilled when it worked perfectly.

She was surprised and delighted that I was able to do it for her, and proudly went round telling everyone what I'd done and what an amazing boy I was. She told me that I was a very creative young man, but that was typical of the way I was already thinking. When my classmates were playing outside, I would often be learning how to do practical things and solve problems, and that has never changed.

I've always been driven to seek a better way of doing things, and I think I can probably trace the success of my business career right back to that day with granny. It was the first time I had used my brain and hands to fix something, and experienced the special thrill of success.

Today, I'm very fortunate to hold dual British and Romanian nationalities, and very proud to be a part of both countries. I've learned many different things from each of them, and they both have rich and varied histories that Simona and I are extremely happy to be able to share with our children.

Unfortunately, however, I wasn't always happy about being Romanian. When I was in school, I was regularly bullied for having what was regarded as a Soviet surname. The other children mocked Voloseniuc for being a Ukrainian name, because we lived on the border of that country which – at the time – was a part of the Soviet Union.

As well as the inevitable cross-fertilisation that occurs between villages and towns that are very close to each other, the region had changed rulers many times during the centuries as the different empires reallocated vast areas of land and people to fit their own political ambitions.

In the minds of my classmates, any country that had been absorbed into the Soviet Union was regarded as Russian. So they would insist that I was not Romanian, and should get out and go back to Russia.

This really was very traumatic for a young boy who already lacked confidence and had few friends. For a period, the bullying had a very negative impact on my development and ability to mix with others.

It also reinforced the sense of being an outsider that I've carried for my whole life. They were telling me that I wasn't good enough, and didn't belong with them. So rather than identify as a Romanian, I just saw myself as Stefan. It was me against the world.

We had classrooms where all the boys and girls were taught together, and as well as the Romanians, there was quite a large grouping of German children. But it was invariably only the small number with Russian or Ukrainian names who were picked on.

Even at that young age, I decided I would do my best to always be better. To be fair and straight with other people, and to care about them. It was very painful at the time, and I loathe bullying in all its forms, but I can now see that having to grow up with that name eventually helped me develop my individuality – and determined much of my later approach to life. I would tell myself that I was Romanian, and was going to make success happen, no matter what they said.

Being poor was also a big driver, as there were sometimes days where we almost had nothing at all to eat.

I resolved that my own children would never have to face that pain and fear. They were tough times.

It wasn't easy to study and concentrate when feeling hungry and being bullied. I would often ask myself why the world was like that? Why could we not have a meal? Why did we rarely have nice clothes? Why did we all have to sleep in the same room?

As I gradually realised that it was largely because of the decisions that someone else had taken, my questions changed from negatives to positives. I asked myself why I shouldn't also have a nice lifestyle, be able to go to good restaurants, drive a new car, and look after my family. It forced me to get out of the mindset that had gripped so many in my village, and was an essential part of my young development.

After centuries of oppression, there were many people around me who had a naturally pessimistic mindset. I now think that, although I was too young to realise it, this negative culture also sowed the seeds of my interest in politics – as well as my determination that one day I wanted to be in a position where I could make a difference. I wanted to help future generations of Romanian children to have a happier and more fulfilling childhood.

My attitude has always been that the only way to make progress and find success is to try new things, and not be afraid to take risks. We all know that not everything we attempt will come off. There will be lots of mistakes and failures, and I certainly have a few of those on my business CV. But the old clichés are true, and if nothing is ventured then nothing is gained.

It still annoys me when I hear people moan with jealousy when they see someone else's success – and yet they have never actually tried to do, create, or start something themselves. If you try ten things and just one of them comes off and earns you money and happiness, then you will be satisfied that you have done something with your life. That is what I have tried to teach my own children.

The world is obsessed with identity politics at the moment, and I know that a lot of my family were indeed Ukrainian or Russian. But of course I feel Romanian because I was born in Romania and I have Romanian citizenship. I certainly don't feel less than any other nationality.

I am equally proud that my children were born in England and that I am an adopted Englishman through naturalisation. I see that as an honour because I think England is one of the best countries on Earth.

But where we are born is never our choice, which is why no-one should feel superior than others based purely on their birthplace. I wouldn't be what I am now if it wasn't for the English mentality and approach to life.

I arrived in London with nothing except a few pounds, a contact name, and some natural determination. But this country welcomed me, allowed me to create my own opportunities, and gave me a landscape so that I could find and build myself.

When I discuss this with my Romanian friends, I ask them to imagine how different life could be for future Romanian generations if only their politicians could offer young people the same opportunities and encouragement that I've found in London.

As I write this book there are many problems in the UK with the cost of living crisis, high inflation, rising interest rates and astonishing rises in the cost of fuel and energy. Those, and other issues, are having a major effect on our family and business. And yet, despite all the difficulties, there is still an optimism and faith that we will work through the situation as a nation – a feeling that I have not found in Romania.

I am, and always will be, a Romanian in my heart, despite the attempts of certain classmates to make me think otherwise. I hope that the millions in our diaspora who are scattered around the world can be a wonderful resource in the future, and that a way is found to harness their skills and experiences for the benefit of the nation of our birth.

The date of my birth, August 23, was also the day of the annual celebration of the Communist Party. On that day, we all had to dress in the same colour with blue shirts and a tie in the Romanian colours at school, and stand together to sing the national anthem.

It was obviously brainwashing, but it was also fun at the time – and as it was my birthday I used to feel a little bit special as well. I suspect that these ceremonies must have come to an end after Ceausescu was executed.

My other recollections from that time are quite sketchy, but as we didn't have any local pre-school facilities I first went to a village school in Izvoarele Sucevei for about a year when I was five. I remember that in the winter I went to stay with my cousins, and we had to wake up when it was still dark and walk through the snow.

We could hear dogs angrily barking in nearby gardens, and it was quite scary. It was probably only a couple of kilometres, but at that age it felt as though we were crossing a continent.

The morning lessons ran from 8am till noon, and we had a wood burning fire in the classroom to warm us up and help dry our sodden clothing and shoes. We then had a lunch that we'd brought from home, and more classes in the afternoon.

When my parents moved back to my grandparents' house in 1989, I went to a primary school about 4km away at Tibao for a year. Then, when we moved to our main house in the centre of Cârlibaba, I went to the school that was immediately next door. Which was where I stayed until I was 14.

After that, I went to an academy in Nasaud called the Nasaud Forestry High School for four years. It was about 100km from home, and halfway between Suceava and Cluj. I spent the first two years living with Ana Maria, and the final ones with my younger sister, Stefania.

We lived in a small room with two single beds in a communal house that was about half-an-hour's walk from the academy. It wasn't a great part of the city, but was the closest that our parents could afford to rent for us. If the weather was bad, the roads were a wet and muddy nightmare to negotiate.

We shared a kitchen and bathroom with an older lady and her niece, but I was very lucky during the first two years as Ana Maria took charge. She would cook for me, have my clothes cleaned and ensure that everything was in order. She is a very intelligent woman who went to Oradea University on the Hungarian border to study civil engineering after she finished her qualifications in Nasaud.

In her final year there, she met a married Greek Catholic priest and had a child with him, which initially caused a few problems with all the different families. But they later got married themselves, and now have four children and live back in Suceava.

When Stefania arrived to study at the academy, it was a nightmare period for both of us as we didn't get on very well and had very different attitudes to the living arrangements. I even threatened to kick her out of the house if she didn't cook my food, as at that age I didn't know how to do anything for myself, and was fed up that I seemed to be having fried eggs or sausages every day!

I would not be happy if my sons spoke to their sister like that now, but during that period Romania was still a very male-dominated society, and the sisters were expected to look after the men in their family. I also don't think I'd ever try that with Steffi again, as she went to the army academy after leaving school and is now a senior officer in the Romanian army.

Regrettably, we had a big falling out when we were young, which is not surprising when I think about the conditions and circumstances we grew up in. But she did help me with a loan when I left for Portugal that I was very grateful for, although she probably just wanted to make sure I stayed out of the country!

We are all very proud of what she has achieved, and she combines work with being a wife to Marius and a mother to two children. They are a lovely family and we are now much closer.

I was studying for the Forestry Commission when I was at the academy, because it was always dad's dream that

I would take his place, but I really didn't like school and had no interest in most of the subjects.

I was ok with geometry but struggled with things like history and physics and also Romanian, as it is a very complicated language. At that time, I also had no interest in learning Russian and French, which seems strange as I later discovered I was able to pick up new languages very easily.

We were sometimes taught about Romanian art and culture, and studied writers and poets such as Mihai Eminescu, but we were told very little about the rest of the world because the educational system was still emerging from the years of rigid communist educational plans and curriculums.

There were, however, two subjects that I enjoyed and put a lot of time into: sport and engineering. I loved sport, especially football and athletics. I was very good at middle-distance running, and was definitely someone who preferred being in the open air as opposed to spending days stuck in classrooms.

I also enjoyed studying engineering, as it was the only lesson I found to be stimulating and useful in all my years at school. I'm sure that helped lead me to where I am now, because from the very beginning I enjoyed learning about building roads and getting the levels and curves right.

That was something that stuck in my mind many years later when I was starting out in London. I knew what needed to be done for the water to run off properly when we were planning work, and that impressed my supervisors.

We also learned a range of other related disciplines, including topography and surveying, and lots of things that were important for working in the forests, such as how to measure trees and the different processes of logging and tree management.

But it was the building process that truly captured my mind. I was fascinated by the whole process of construction, and the excitement that comes from creating something out of nothing. Of taking a small idea and seeing it grow until it becomes a house, a block of flats, a new road, or a company that provides work for hundreds of people.

I have to admit that I wasn't the best of students. Six months before my final fourth-year exams, I was getting some disappointingly average marks of 55 to 65 percent. I began to get very concerned, because I was dreading failing and returning home to face my dad. I didn't want to admit that I'd wasted my time and his money, so I got my head down and studied harder than at any time in my life.

I read everything I could, but as I'd missed many lectures I had to bribe my friends with pizza to get them to lend me their notes. Fortunately, it paid off. When the final results were announced, I had achieved my baccalaureate and come third in my form of more than twenty students.

My form teacher was shocked, as he knew I'd spent very little time in class, but I knew that when I really set my mind to something I can do it – even if it meant that I also increased the profits of all the local pizza cafés in the town!

I had a similar experience when I gained my British nationality. I had been so busy working that I'd had little time to study the documents I needed to learn. I waited until a couple of days before the exam before I even started doing the tests online, but I was determined to achieve the citizenship at the first attempt and sat up for much of the night revising – and also drinking a few pints as I worked.

The next day, despite being hungover, I went to the test centre. As I checked in, I noticed there were lots of people in the room from different backgrounds. It drove home yet again just how many people from around the globe want to become British.

I was feeling very confident, and it probably took me not much more than ten minutes to complete the multiple-choice questions and leave. I was so quick that the invigilator was completely perplexed, and very concerned that maybe I was unwell or had misunderstood what was needed. He kept checking with me that I really wanted to go.

I assured him that all was fine, and that I knew exactly what I was doing, but he still looked very doubtful as he went into the system to check my score. The doubt changed to surprise when he looked up and congratulated me for having passed. Being somewhat arrogant in those days, I told him that of course I had, and that I knew that I was going to, otherwise I wouldn't have wasted my time going there.

Now I have two passports, and am a very proud British citizen. As well as the written test – which was a wide mix of questions about the history, culture, politics and government of the UK – I had to prove that I'd worked and lived here for five years, and not been away from the country for six months at any stage.

Then I swore my pledge to the Queen, and was given a certificate to send to the Home Office to get my passport and become a British citizen. It was a long journey from

Cârlibaba but one that I am very glad I made.

After I finished my studying in Romania, I had no idea what I wanted to do – other than to ensure that I was able to make something good with my life, and achieve it on my own terms. It was hard at first to come up with a strategy, as my dad thought I was being foolish and irresponsible.

His straightforward and unswerving opinion was that you went to school, got a job, lived locally, started a family and worked until you retired. That was it, his entire worldview and his plan for me, and that was why he was so determined to prevent me from leaving Romania.

At first, when I returned to Cârlibaba he encouraged me to apply to a university in Iasi to study law. But it would have been far too expensive, and there were very limited places available. Almost everyone had to pay the fees themselves, unless they had outstanding exam results or a personal political contact who could secure one of the small number of free spots that were quietly reserved for the well-connected.

In addition, my parents were already supporting my brothers and sisters in their education, which was putting a huge strain on their small income, so I made the decision to leave Romania and look for a better life elsewhere.

The first thing I realised I needed to acquire was a driving licence. I knew that would be useful when I was looking for work, and probably essential when I was abroad. By that time, dad had his first car – a small blue Dacia. It was a terrible vehicle, which was just as well as he was a terrible driver and crashed it so often that it looked as though it had come straight from a scrapyard.

He didn't give me lessons himself, thank goodness,

but did generously pay for me to have some at a driving school. I managed to pass my test first time, and have been in love with cars and driving ever since.

I purchased my own first car when I was in Portugal. It was a red Renault 5, the classic old shape. I paid 480 euros to buy it from an old lady. I was so thrilled that I cleaned and polished it almost every day, and even put perfume inside to get rid of some of the historic smells I inherited. I was incredibly happy, and felt as though I had gone up a level in life.

About a year later, I was working for a construction company when the boss helped me buy a VW Vento that was something like seven years old. It was a bigger car, and amazing to drive – but for some reason that is now lost in my memory, I next downgraded to an Opal Corsa before stepping up several notches with an Audi A4 when I moved to London.

I got that one on finance from Cargiant in West London. It was a couple of years old, but was very special to own and drive. I even drove it to Romania on a couple of visits home. After I sold that, I bought a second-hand BMW X5, which was a dream car for a while, but then I traded it for a Mercedes M-Class, before switching to a second-hand BMW X6 for a couple of years.

It was important for me to have a car that looked and felt good, as well as being practical and reliable, but I also knew that at each stage I was showing myself and the world that hard work and determination could produce success. This has enabled me to enjoy the luxuries and cars that I could have only dreamed about as a child whose family used a horse and cart in the mountains and woods.

In 2015, I was thrilled to be able to take a major step up and purchase my first Bentley. I'd been looking for the right one for some time, since one of my friends had taken me for a drive in his. I was astonished at the impressive hand-finishing, and attention to the smallest details. When I was finally able to purchase a new blue GTC Convertible on finance, it was an incredible experience.

I switched that for a normal Bentley, and then in 2017 I bought a four-year-old Rolls Royce Ghost. Despite my previous rapid turnover of vehicles, I've still got it seven years later and love everything about such a wonderful and perfectly built car.

With the finance deals available in the UK, it is very easy to own and upgrade cars on a regular basis. But I just love them, and as I spend so much time at work, motoring is the one hobby I allow myself to indulge in.

5

Portugal

It was a massive step to leave home in 2002, at just 19. But it was something I knew I had to do for myself, as I had already recognised there were going to be very few opportunities for me to grow and develop in Romania.

Before beginning my life-changing adventure, I had thought about it for many months. But my information was extremely limited. At that time, we had no internet nor smartphones, and my knowledge of the outside world was narrow.

I also had to consider the feelings of my father. I knew he'd feel betrayed because he had always been very open about how desperately he wanted – and fully expected – his eldest son to remain at home and follow him into his forestry work.

The mindset of my father's generation was still that of the Ceausescu era, when people worried all the time about the security of their jobs and income. Life was, and in many ways still is, so politicised that work was used as patronage and leverage. Ruthless and corrupt – and often very lazy – politicians would hand out jobs to their friends and family as favours.

My father never gave me money, as he was scared I'd save it up and use it to leave home. But that approach only increased my determination to find some independence. I had a strong desire to strike out on my own, and see what the wider world could offer me.

My first destination came about because of a random conversation in early 2002, rather than through a careful grand design. One of my friends from the village, Alex Dranca, had recently returned home from working in Portugal.

One evening when we sat in a local bar talking about life and our plans and ambitions, he encouraged me to follow his example and head to Lisbon, as I would be able to work and study there if I was serious about getting away from Cârlibaba.

Alex also very kindly offered to help me find a job and accommodation, and teach me the language, so I enthusiastically accepted. I had nothing to lose. Even if things didn't work out, I knew that at the very least I'd gain some valuable life experience. And I would still have the option of returning home to the forest.

It was the biggest and most important decision of my life. I was very excited, especially as I'd always wanted to study civil engineering, and he explained that it should be fairly straightforward for me to enrol in a Portuguese college once I'd settled in.

Having made up my mind to leave, I then faced the challenge of working out how I could actually do it. Talking and dreaming were easy, but I had very little money. Lisbon was more than 3500km away, which seemed rather too far to hitch or walk. There was only one thing to do. As so often in my life, I went to see my granny and asked for her advice.

She sat and quietly listened as I poured out my concerns and confusion and ambitions. Then she took my hands in hers and said that, although she would miss me very badly, she understood why I wanted to move to Portugal. She thought it was a good idea, and definitely the right step for me at that stage in my life.

She then went to a box that was hidden at the back of a cupboard in her kitchen, took out some money, and gave it to me with the words '*Stefan, this will help you get there but remember that I will need it to be repaid as it is the money I have saved for my funeral.*'

I gave her a big hug, thanked her, and promised I would repay the money – while also reminding her that she was only in her early 60s and had many years ahead of her yet! My family have always loved to be dramatic. My sister Stefania also very kindly lent me some money. Combining these loans with the small savings I had also kept to one side, I was able to plan my escape.

I decided to leave home in February 2002. I chose the day carefully as my dad was working away from the village. Mum knew and fully accepted my determination to leave. She helped me pack and go to the bus stop, but my dad had no idea what I was about to do. If he had, I know he'd have taken away my ID to prevent me from travelling.

I was later told that, when he returned home that evening, he was shocked when he couldn't find me. He simply hadn't believed that I would ever have the inner courage to actually go.

Apparently he slumped onto a chair and wept, and asked over and over again how I could do this to him. He was very unhappy, but I suspect that was as much to do with his recognition that he could no longer control my life as it was with my absence.

I was the first of his children to leave home, and when we spoke on the phone a few days later, he begged me to return. But by then I was enjoying the first chance in my life to be free to make my own decisions. In my dad's eyes, I was abandoning him, but in mine I was escaping from a place that would limit my chances to develop.

The bus journey to Portugal took me through Hungary, Austria, Germany, Belgium, France and Spain. It lasted three days and three very long nights. When I finally arrived at Alex's place at around 4am, I was shattered, and my legs were cramped and hurting.

I managed to get a couple of hours sleep, then went straight to a job interview that had been arranged for me, and was asked to start almost immediately. Initially, I stayed with Alex and his friends for three months in a flat about 100km from Lisbon, and near to a coastal town called Peniche.

It was very nice, with four bedrooms, two bathrooms, a kitchen and a balcony. There were usually four or five of us living there. Having saved some money, I later moved into a bigger flat with a few other guys I'd met.

Now I had my own room in the penthouse. After

spending the majority of my life sharing a bedroom with my siblings, this was like heaven for me. The job, on the other hand, was like hell.

I was working at a nearby farm, and it was just awful. We woke up at 5.30am each morning for coffee and breakfast, as we had to be on site no later than 6.30am to start loading trucks with empty boxes.

The women arrived an hour later, and then we'd all go to the fields together to begin our day of picking cabbages and onions, with the girls moving in front of us to cut them whilst the guys followed with two boxes each that we'd fill and then carry the 200m or 300m back to the truck.

We'd do that for the whole morning, and it was almost indescribably tedious as well as being physically extremely tiring. The early chat and banter soon dried up, as we all became lost in our thoughts and dreams.

We couldn't afford the recently launched iPods, and it was still a long time before the development of iPhones, so we had no radio or music to listen to – just the sound of cabbages being cut and our own souls withering with boredom.

Because it was February, it was cold and wet, and there was a lot of mud. So much mud. More mud than I think must have existed in the whole of Cârlibaba, and there were times when I thought about my father's experience in the muddy fields of his childhood. At least – unlike him – I had boots to protect my feet.

Our afternoons were spent in the warehouse, where, for the next stage in the process, we had to sort, wash, size and pack the produce and then clean the pallets. Most days we didn't finish much before 10pm because, as well as his own farm, the owner collected vegetables from other farmers and fields, and we had to process those as well.

There were probably 50 people working in that farm: a real mix of nationalities featuring not only Portuguese but also Romanians, Ukrainians, Russians and Kosovars. Regardless of our nationality, we were treated as slaves and expected to work for 14 or 15 hours a day while earning a paltry 2.50 Euros an hour.

We had Sundays off, and occasionally Saturday afternoons were free, but I started to pray that I'd soon find an alternative job as I felt that it was all so unfair and more like modern slavery.

The guy who owned the farm was usually very unpleasant to us, but I was ambitious and competitive and didn't want to give him an excuse to rant and swear at me. In fact, I worked so hard that there were times when blood poured from my nose because of the pressure I was putting myself under.

The owner must have noticed and liked me, because after one month at the farm he gave me a surprise pay rise. When, a couple of months after that, I told him I was leaving to take a job on a construction site, he tried hard to persuade me to stay, and even offered me a full-time job.

The experience of working in those fields was deeply unpleasant, but it did mean that for the first time I was able to empathise with those who are doing the hidden jobs in our society.

In every country there will be men, women and sometimes children who are employed in the dirty, difficult, boring, repetitious and low-paid jobs that enable the rest of us to enjoy a nice lifestyle and food. It is very important that we recognise that, and respect them for what they do.

Here was also a very good early example of how not to treat people when they are working for you. I saw and felt for myself what it was like to work for someone who was rude and selfish, and just didn't care at all about the health of his team.

That made a very big mark on me, and is one of the reasons why I take the approach I do in my different businesses, where the mental and physical wellbeing of the staff is at the centre of our planning and management.

After three months encased in mud, I heard from friends about a construction job in a small village called Ferrel. It was with a company called Antonio de Santos Ltd, and I was so happy when I was accepted.

The first day almost felt as though I was on a holiday break, because the standard working hours were between 8am and 5pm. I couldn't believe it when the day ended so early, compared with my previous experience.

I had become used to working 14 hours a day, and eating so little food that I had even become quite skinny. It was a major boost for my health to work decent hours, and be able to eat and rest properly.

I had also specifically wanted to work in construction, as I was anxious to develop and learn new things – and that was never going to happen in agriculture, where the available stimulation from cutting cabbages was limited.

Even at that young age, and as a very unworldly teenager, I was already looking ahead and developing ambitions. I always thought that if I could learn the correct way to build a wall or dig a foundation properly, I would be in a position to work hard and earn some good money. Then, maybe one day, I could have my own business and employ other people.

As I look back now, I am astonished at how confident, determined and calm I was. I'm not sure that it ever really occurred to me that I might fail. I don't mean that I was arrogant – because I wasn't. At least, no more than any 19-year-old is.

And yet, having taken the big decision to leave Romania, I could see a very clear path in front of me. I was becoming aware of the enormous opportunities that were available to millions of other young people across Europe, who weren't carrying the burden of decades of communism, and the low expectations that were invariably felt by those who were born or grew up under regimes such as Ceausescu's.

I stayed in touch with home whenever I could, although that was still a time when phone cards were the only real way of making calls across Europe. I could only usually afford to spend 10 or 15 Euros, and would sometimes lose my cards, but tried to call my family whenever possible. Mum always wanted to know my news, but my dad tended to stay in the background as he was still disappointed I'd left.

One of the most amazing things that happened to me during this period was the unexpected discovery that I was naturally good at languages. We'd never had much chance to learn them at school, as there were few opportunities to use them, and almost all travel was banned. It felt so daunting when I arrived in Portugal, went to a bar on my first night, and heard people speak these strange words.

I was shocked, and thought I'd never be able to speak Portuguese, but I managed to pick it up very quickly as I was surrounded by it on TV and at work. In fact, more than 20 years later, I can still speak it now.

I was fast becoming a new man, and already very different from the naïve teenager who had got on a bus in northern Romania at the start of 2002. Within six months, I had learned the language, was living in a nice apartment with good friends, earning decent money in a job I enjoyed, and had my first girlfriend. I was very happy.

The next few months were spent working on different sites, going to the gym, and enjoying life with my new friends. I moved to Lisbon in spring 2003 to work with a different company, and settled easily and happily into the next stage of life.

Because I was a long way from home, and didn't know many people outside of work, I joined a nearby gym to use in the evenings when I first arrived. I wanted to build up my muscles. People used to think I must be a boxer because of my physique and shape, but I was no more able to fight or defend myself than I had been when I was as a kid, as I'd never been trained.

That was brought home to me very violently in Christmas 2003, when a group of us went to a party at a bar in Lisbon. I don't recall the name, or exactly where it was, but I know we were having a lot of fun, and it was very relaxing with people dancing and celebrating.

Unfortunately, as is so often the case, there was one guy who was extremely drunk and causing a lot of problems.

He was Romanian. I felt a responsibility to sort out

the situation, so I grabbed him and managed to get him outside the building and into the alleyway. He was almost incoherent, but continued to shout and swear at me as he lurched backwards when I released his arms.

It sounded as though he was threatening me, but I told him to go home and behave himself. Then I went back inside to rejoin my friends, and thought no more of it.

At 2.30am, I finally decided it was time to leave, so I said my goodbyes, wished everyone a happy Christmas, and slowly made my way outside into the shock of the cold morning air. As my blurred and tired eyes began to acclimatise to the lights on the street, I became aware of a shape moving quickly towards me.

My brain was just awake enough to realise it was the same guy I'd thrown out a few hours earlier. As I assumed he was trying to slap me, I leaned forward to take and break the blow.

Unfortunately, my brain was not quite awake enough to see that he was also holding a broken champagne bottle. It was a horrible shock when it connected with my skull, and left me with a long and ragged cut from my right ear to the back of my head.

I fell to the floor in a growing pool of blood, and my world-view changed for ever. I have a recollection of lying on my side on the ground, but being unable to move as I drifted in and out of consciousness. Someone called an ambulance, but it took 40 minutes to arrive and transfer me to a nearby hospital. During that period, I lost a lot of blood.

It was the only time in my life when I genuinely thought I was going to die. I could hear the medics saying they were not sure I was going to make it. It was as though I was suddenly in a distant bubble with my own thoughts, almost drifting away from the world. My whole body seemed to be paralysed. I lay there in silence, feeling a deep fear of the darkness that seemed to be steadily edging towards me.

There was a window in the ambulance roof. Through it I could see the stars in the December sky, and I can remember thinking that this was a ridiculous situation and so unfair. I had come to Lisbon to give myself the chance of a better life. Now I was dying at the hands of a drunk from my own country.

That wasn't right. In my mind, I told God that I wasn't ready. I begged and prayed that he would not take me in that moment. I had so much more that I wanted to do in my life. I was missing my family, as I hadn't seen my mum or brothers for almost two years, and so I challenged God that – if he existed – we could perhaps do a deal. I even told Him that, if he would just save me and give me another opportunity, I'd become a monk!

My friends came to the hospital to offer me support when I was taken straight into surgery to be given blood and get stitched up. The doctors were incredible. After I'd come round properly, they told me how lucky I was to be alive. Most people who sustain a serious injury in that place on the head rarely survive, as they lose so much blood.

As for the man who hit me, I have no idea. He was tall and skinny and ran off as soon as I went down. I never saw him again, but he made me determined to ensure that if I ever faced a similar problem, I would know exactly how to defend myself.

It took many months to completely recover from the assault, because I often suffered from dizzy spells and anxiety attacks, and it was a while before I became fully confident again. But during that period I did a lot of online research about boxing and training, and started planning ahead.

Following my final set of tests and scans, the doctors confirmed that my injuries had healed and my brain was, thankfully, unaffected. They agreed they were happy for me to join a gym and train to box.

I loved it, and the experience immediately brought me back to life. I thrived on learning the technical side of the sport, and really got into the movements and training. I was probably around 75kg, and looked like a middleweight. I was fast, and trained several times a week with a new purpose in life, even if it wasn't quite the same as joining a monastery as I had promised in my last-gasp bargain.

Around the same time, I had come across another friend from home, Iosif Longier, and moved in with him and his friends. They worked for a company who were building roads and bridges, and they helped me a lot. We lived initially in Setubal and then Caldas da Rainha, where I finally started a civil engineering course.

But I found it difficult to keep up with the coursework because of all the other distractions. I realised that learning new skills at work would be more valuable than a formal qualification, and I have never regretted that decision.

It was around this time that I probably hit my sporting peak. I began regularly playing football again, as I wanted something extra to do in the evenings having split from my then girlfriend.

I had always been passionate about the sport, and followed Steaua Bucharest – the side that had dominated Romania for almost my entire life up to that point. At school, I'd been a good attacking midfielder who also scored on a regular basis, and for a while I'd had dreams about making it my career.

When I was 14, I badly wanted to attend Bistrita High School to be a part of their renowned sports programme and play football, but my dad was strongly against that and refused to let me apply. Instead – and to my disbelieving horror – I found myself being enrolled in the National Military College in Alba Iulia.

It was one of the worst periods of my life, as I very quickly discovered that I was not meant to be a soldier. After two miserable weeks as a cadet, I deliberately failed my preliminary exam and managed to persuade dad to collect me. I have great admiration for the men and women of our armed forces, but I had no wish to join them and spend my teenage years marching around a parade ground.

Caldas da Rainha FC were in the Portuguese third division, although they were struggling with their finances and had a small squad. I had a trial with them, and the three directors who watched me said they were impressed by my potential as a 21-year-old.

They suggested I spend a few weeks training with their juniors in the evenings and weekends, so I could develop my skills and speed before moving into the senior squad. Throughout February and March 2005, the coaches put me through the toughest regime I'd ever experienced.

I was astonished to discover how quickly my speed, ball skills and muscle memory improved. The kids I was playing with were so good because they had started at a young age and had massive leg muscles, and our training matches were tough and often bloody. It was very hard work, and there were times when I was leaving the training camp in my car that I'd notice I had double vision because of the pressure I was putting my body through.

Once a week, we also had games with the senior team which were competitive and intense, – not least because the groundsman would water the pitch just before we'd play. That forced us to concentrate on close control. As soon as you received a pass, if you didn't know how to stop the ball, it would run very fast because of the water, and it could be easy to lose possession.

I settled in straight away with my new team-mates, and managed to impress the coach and directors with my goal-scoring and positional play. As well as looking to score myself, I would pass lots of balls into good positions for others.

One evening at the end of the season, they called me aside. They congratulated me on the effort I'd been putting in, and assured me that, when the new season began in August, I'd be in the first-team squad.

That was great to hear. Unfortunately, destiny then intervened and decided that I wasn't going to become a top international footballer and lead Romania to World Cup glory. There were two main reasons for my decision to decline their kind offer.

The first was the request by the club for me to contribute 50 per cent towards the fee to get my licence from the Football Association. It usually cost something like 3000 Euros, which I didn't have.

There was a logical reason behind the club asking for a deposit, as they'd had problems in the past when they'd paid for a licence and the player then either didn't train or play for them, so they wanted to see my contribution and know that I was committed.

This opportunity also coincided with my father's decision to retire from his job in the forest. He made it clear that he expected me to do my duty as the eldest son, forget my silly ideas of working abroad, and return home to inherit his position – as was so often still the tradition in Romania.

Feeling unhappy and confused about what I wanted for myself and my life, I turned down the club's offer, handed in my notice at the site, and very reluctantly returned to Cârlibaba.

I left everything behind, gifting my car and TV and belongings to my friends as I no longer wanted any of it. I obviously hadn't yet developed the mind of a businessman as I gave it all away for free.

However, I almost immediately regretted making that decision, and knew it had been a foolish one. I'd built a good life for myself in Portugal, where I had a home and was settling in with a good group of friends.

Instead, I gave up everything and went home to my father, who had worn me down by relentless nagging whenever we spoke on the phone. Eventually, I came to feel that I had an obligation to him and my family. And that there was no other option other to accept the inevitable.

This was the end of my fledgling football career. Although, when I occasionally managed to play in some local matches when I was back living with my parents, I was startled to discover how much more advanced my game had become compared to my former schoolfriends.

I could get several metres' advantage very quickly, and put the ball up front, but unfortunately it was to prove a mixed blessing as it was almost always too fast for the forwards to react.

It was a different story with boxing, because it was now in my blood and I really cared for the sport. My good friend Sorin Popescu and I trained almost every day in our own improvised gym, that we set up in his house with buckets of rock and sand combined with cables and wood. Sorin later married my wife's sister, so we are still able to talk about the sport and imagine the championships we could have won!

Jumping ahead slightly, when I eventually moved to London a couple of years later, I was told about the famous All Stars Boxing Gym on the Harrow Road that had been started by the inspirational Isola Akay in 1974. Numerous legends have trained at this grounded community club, including world champions Joe Calzaghe, Frank Bruno, Nigel Benn, Evander Holyfield, and my all-time boxing hero Mike Tyson.

To even be standing in the same changing-room and ring that Tyson had used was a big thrill. Today, I have a signed boxing glove and pair of his shorts framed in my office on the wall behind my desk that Cliff, a very good friend, generously gave me as a present.

I joined the All Stars Gym, and was soon training obsessively several times a week and really throwing myself into the sport. After a while, I caught the eye of one of the trainers who said he thought I was ready to start taking some fights.

But, as with the football, I had to stop going along as I just didn't have the time with the way my work was developing. That was a real pity, as I think I'd have been good, especially as I am so focused on everything I ever do, but I had to concentrate on my business career at that stage.

However, a new world had opened up to me. I have so much admiration for boxers and trainers and their whole community. I like almost everything about the sport. The movement, the opportunities, the punches and the respect. I learned that it's not so much about fighting as calculation, technical ability and footwork. It is an art.

I love watching boxing on TV, although that was rarely possible when I was in Romania, even though we had some world champions of our own including Francisc Vastag, Leonard Doroftei and Lucian Bute, whose nephew Tudore Bute worked with me for a period in London.

I also now try and watch live bouts when I can, although I admit that the first time I was ringside I was shocked at how real the blood and sweat suddenly seemed. I'd never really noticed it when I was training and sparring, but as an audience member it felt very different, and the sounds of the contest and the crowd just added to the drama.

In September 2018, I was able to get tickets with a good view of the ring at Wembley Stadium to watch Britain's world heavyweight champion Anthony Joshua stop Russia's Alexander Povetkin in the seventh round. That was a thrilling fight. I was there with friends and had an amazing time.

I had a personal reason to be happy for Joshua. After abandoning my regular training in 2008 when I started my business, I went along to the Finchley ABC gym during the following year. It was close to where I was living in Edgware – and, for a while, I was part of the same group as AJ, who were trained by the legendary Sean Murphy.

I remember AJ as a tall skinny guy, who had been in a bit of trouble, and was encouraged to train by his cousin. So it was very exciting to follow his career, and watch his gold medal triumph at the 2012 London Olympic Games. And even better when he won so many of the heavyweight world title belts to become world champion.

The heavyweight title has long been called the greatest prize in sport. There are few people who can have deserved it more than AJ, as he's a very decent and down-to-earth man. I was particularly happy to see him win on that night at Wembley, as I collected more than £1000 on a bet I'd made on the fight!

But let's return to Bukovina, where it didn't take me long to realise that heading home from Portugal had been a very bad idea. I was a completely different person to the young man who had left the village a few years before, and after the excitement of my life in Lisbon with all my new friends, Cârlibaba seemed very dull by comparison.

I also missed the money, as I'd been earning some good wages in construction, and had relished being financially independent for the first time in my life. Now I was faced with an unwelcome alternative reality of Romanian woods, comparative poverty, and decades of restriction. I knew that I had to return to Lisbon as, like so many millions of young Romanians during this period who left the country, I could see no other way forward.

I stayed in Romania for several months to help my parents, and waited until the first snow as I knew that life would largely come to a stop while the ground was blanketed in white. This time there was no subterfuge. I was very open about my plans to leave for a second time, and made it very clear that I wouldn't be talked out of it.

I was, however, very apprehensive and embarrassed. I thought my friends and former colleagues would ridicule me as a failure if, having left my job and given away all my belongings, I returned to Lisbon with my tail between my legs.

But they instantly welcomed me back, and even though I was starting all over again, I knew that this time I had left Romania for good. I had decisively joined the gigantic diaspora of people who were seeking new lives and adventures across Europe.

Fortunately, I got my old job back with the same company, and it went so well that my boss even gave me a pay rise – which was great for my self-confidence as well as my bank balance. As a result, I was finally able to rent my own home. A few months later, my brother Ilie came to live with me as well, so it was lovely to have family as well as friends in my life.

I was working on construction sites, mainly as a crane operator, which was surprisingly easy, despite my lack of experience. I only had a couple of days training before starting and, not surprisingly, I almost smashed a few roofs. But I soon worked out how to operate the levers.

You have to control the turnaround and the balance at the same time, and that can be tricky to get right, but I was pretty good and they liked me. I was soon responsible for delivering large items from one site to another. It was the perfect role for me at that time: good income with regular hours, and I didn't have to do any hard labour or physical work.

My company worked on a wide range of projects including roads, bridges and apartments, and I made some very good Portuguese friends whom I still stay in touch with. One of them was even kind enough to send me money when I was struggling at one stage in England.

My only problem was that I was still restless, and looking for an opportunity to travel to a country where it would be easier to start my own company and achieve my longer-term ambitions.

I was always looking around, and seeing how it could be done better. I do that even now. Sometimes I'm wrong, and I know I'm not perfect, but I try to learn. What I know is that, if you work hard and are honest to yourself, you will always succeed.

You have to be a realist, and get the right information, which is why I knew it would be difficult to start my own business in Portugal. They had very conservative views, and wouldn't have given me the same opportunities that I have enjoyed in England. As usual, I didn't have a plan. But, thanks once again to a chance meeting, I had the unexpected option of a move to Paris.

6

Paris

I was working in Portugal on a building site, next to the home of a very friendly older lady called Mrs Santos who had three energetic dogs that she'd take out for exercise every day. As we were onsite for several weeks, we used to wave and say hello. Gradually, I got to know her well enough to help carry her bags from the car when she'd been shopping.

Sometimes she'd ask for assistance with walking her dogs, and as we steadily built a friendship, she'd often bring me coffee and cookies in the morning. One day she asked if I could also help her with some jobs in her garden on the following Saturday, and offered to pay me.

Because she was so kind, and the additional income was undoubtedly useful, I agreed and turned up that weekend to start digging and weeding and cutting back some branches of her trees and bushes. When I paused for a break, she made us both some lunch and proudly told me about her son Jose who was a successful entrepreneur, having moved to France and established his own construction business in Paris.

I must have seemed interested in his story, as she called him there and then, and handed me the phone to speak with him. Although he was a little surprised at this unexpected conversation with a Romanian stranger in his mother's house, he said that if I was ever interested in working with him, I should let him know.

Having been in Portugal for a year, I felt I was ready for a new challenge. So, after a few more conversations with Jose during the following weeks, I took up his offer. In the spring of 2006, I booked my coach ticket to once again head off across Europe for a new adventure.

I'll never forget the day I arrived in Paris. I was very excited, and the city was so much bigger than anywhere I'd ever been before. Jose had kindly arranged for my accommodation in Palaiseau, and when I was on the final stages of the coach journey, he called to ask where we had reached.

I looked out of the window and saw we were passing an enormous store called Carrefour. It was so imposing I automatically assumed it must be such a famous Parisian landmark that Jose would know exactly where I was. His sarcastic response made me realise that there were hundreds of Carrefour stores in France!

After I arrived in the terminus, I was taken to a house where a dozen Portuguese workers lived, and introduced to my new set of workmates. As I sat on my bed, I reflected on the fact that I had made yet another major life change with very little planning.

For the second time, I was in a country and city I knew nothing about, and faced with a language I couldn't speak. I was now 23, and at that age I felt invincible, which was just as well as I had a lot to learn.

The reality of Paris was a big shock. I discovered the city and metro were unlike anything I'd ever previously experienced. It felt as though I was inside one of those traditional sets of Russian dolls, where a very small figure is placed inside siblings that get progressively larger.

Everything was bigger, faster and more congested, but fortunately someone was available to cook for us at the house, so I didn't need to go out much in the first few days while I settled in.

When I began work, Jose initially sent me to a site where the other workers were all Portuguese, which came as a big relief as I was at least able to speak with them, even if I had no idea what any of the French street signs said.

They were a good group of people. We were all young and competitive, and knew that if we developed our skills to become decent masons, it was possible to make a lot more money. So we each sought out the best jobs on the site.

My first main job was at one of the biggest children's hospitals in Paris, the Hospital Robert Debre, where a new ward was being built. I was given the address near to the Porte Des Lilas metro station and set off from my apartment in a state of anxiety.

As my only previous experience of an underground network had been in Bucharest, on the occasion when my dad marched his brood into the government offices, the realisation that I would have to travel alone on the Paris metro was a daunting experience. I was scared.

That initial trip involved using a bus, a train and two underground stations. As I spoke no French, I became hopelessly lost and arrived three hours late. No-one had told me how to use the metro, and it was extremely unnerving. I was shocked at how complicated everything was, and ended up in tears.

The day didn't improve when I was met by the Portuguese man in charge of the site. I immediately discovered he was extremely unhappy to have been sent a young Romanian. He was unrelentingly nasty to me, shouting that I was too young to be a mason, and was going to be nothing but a problem for him and one he didn't want.

He then allocated me the most unpleasant jobs as a cleaner and dogsbody for the rest of the team, which was not the welcome I was hoping for on my first day at work.

Having travelled so far, I decided that this time – unlike when I encountered the bullying farmer in Portugal – I had to do my best to keep my mouth shut. I would just stay calm and accept his rudeness and abuse, in the hope that things would improve once the rest of the guys got to know me.

Thankfully, although he remained deeply unpleasant, that proved to be the right approach. Over the coming weeks and months, I met some decent men and started to learn more about the trade. The situation was also helped when I was given my first cheque and it came to almost 3000 Euros for the month – more than double the amount I'd been earning in Portugal.

I quickly began to pick up some basic French, and also to make some new friends and enjoy this latest stage of my life in Paris. Plus, I found a local Romanian church that I began to attend on Sundays. I enjoyed the opportunity to have some quiet time to reflect, as the rest of my life was so relentlessly busy.

The congregation were mainly a lot older than me. Some of them were amused that a young man would join them each weekend, as that was a very unusual occurrence. But they were always welcoming and friendly. As my confidence grew, I began to relax, and got to know more about their stories and backgrounds and learn of the growing diaspora.

One of them was a quiet and distinguished-looking lady who stood out because she always wore colourful and traditional Romanian dress, which was not exactly a common sight in a Parisian suburb.

I discovered that she was the mother of one of my new friends. As she lived very near to where I was staying, and had trouble with her legs, I would sometimes help her on and off the bus if we were travelling at the same time.

One Sunday lunchtime, as we left the church, she invited me to a barbecue she was cooking in her garden for some friends that afternoon. While there, I met another of her sons – Vasile – who told me how lots of his friends had moved to London, as there was so much work and they were paid weekly.

That got me thinking again, wondering if I should make yet another move and try out a third country. It did seem like a very Romanian thing to do – and also as if it might even have been my destiny, because I had reached a point where everything was happening in threes.

Three older ladies had been essential to my travels. My grandma in Romania who lent me the money to leave home, Mrs Santos in Portugal who introduced me to her son in Paris, and now Mrs Mamuca, whose unexpected barbecue invite led to me being told about the opportunities in London.

Three older ladies, and now three countries. Portugal, France and England. It was almost as though I had fallen into one of the many Romanian folk stories I'd learned about when I was a child. So many of those involved a young man from a poor background setting off on a quest where almost everything came in threes.

There would be three tasks, three golden pomegranates, three dragons, three witches, three wishes, three golden apples, three princes, three princesses. And, of course, Romania consists of the three ancient principalities of Wallachia, Moldavia and Transylvania. Our flag even has three colours: red, yellow and blue.

This was clearly a case of destiny. I was a young prince on a quest. Three old ladies. Three countries. It was meant to be. All I had to do now was travel to London, seek my fortune, and marry my princess almost as soon as I set eyes upon her.

But real life is not a fairy tale, so surely none of that could actually happen. Could it?

7

London

As you will have seen at the start of this book, my arrival in London didn't go quite as smoothly as I had hoped. The truth was that this was only the second time I'd ever flown in a plane, and, having no idea how to book a flight ticket online, I ended up very confused. I also knew almost nothing about Britain, and had taken little notice of what I was told in my geography lessons at school.

When I saw a very cheap flight to Glasgow being advertised, I just assumed it must be near London, and bought it. That was a big mistake, and Iacob – who was very kindly organising everything for me – wasn't especially happy when he discovered where I had landed.

He told me to get a train to London. But as I couldn't speak or read much English, and had never before experienced anything like the strong Glaswegian accents I heard all around me at the airport, I was struggling.

Somehow, I managed to get myself onto a train to Leeds, which is about halfway to London – although still in the north of England. But when I arrived there, the city was shrouded in thick fog. At that point, concerned that I might end up completely lost, Iacob told me to stay exactly where I was while he arranged for a friend to drive there, collect me, and carry me safely to London.

One additional and very frustrating aspect that has stuck in my mind was that the train ticket from Glasgow to Leeds cost me three times as much as the air fare from Paris. So the whole exercise was a painful piece of learning for the young Stefan.

Iacob was a very good man, and a cousin of Vasile, the son of the old lady in Paris. As I mentioned, they had suggested I moved to London, where there was a lot of work, a growing Romanian community, and the added incentive that I would be paid at the end of each week. That was very important for someone who had no money, and needed to be able to plan ahead to pay rent and bills and buy food.

Iacob also kindly arranged for me to stay with some friends of his at a flat in Neasden Lane in North London, not far from the famous Wembley Stadium. Seventeen years later, I'm still living in that area, and have subsequently been joined by hundreds of thousands of Romanian diaspora. There are now Romanian shops and churches and businesses across the region.

Back then, Romanians had only recently started arriving in London, as a result of the freedom of movement that opened up when we joined the European Union in January 2007.

It was a strange and very new world in a city that was even bigger than anything I could have imagined. Eight million people lived in London when I arrived, and there are an estimated nine million now. By comparison, Bucharest has 1.8 million today, and there are only 19 million in the whole of Romania.

London is also probably the most multicultural place on earth, which was a very different experience from Cârlibaba. We had Russians and Germans at home, but it was a dramatic change.

However, I got used to it very quickly, and loved the diversity of faces and languages. We are all human, and it is what we believe that makes us different, not what we look like.

Having said that, in my first few days and weeks that wasn't always my experience in the flat where I was suddenly living with people I didn't know anything about – even though they did at least speak my language. Initially, they didn't trust me, and were very wary because I was blond and called Voloseniuc, so they thought I must be Russian.

They were very careful around me, and didn't want to leave me alone in the house in case I stole their money and cars. It wasn't until Iacob was able to speak with Vasile again that they relaxed slightly. Jacob then assured them they could trust me, and that I was a nice guy. There were seven of us living in the house, and I shared a room with two brothers, so it was a bit cramped, but we had proper beds and at least it was fairly clean and warm.

I was so nervous of upsetting them that I wouldn't take anything from the fridge or cupboards, even when they offered to share with me, in case they thought I was going to steal their belongings. It wasn't an easy introduction to London life, and initially I found it very stressful. But eventually I felt more at home, and the others kept a look out for jobs for me.

When I had been there a few weeks, we had a barbecue and a few beers in our back garden during the Easter holiday weekend. As I relaxed, I confidently predicted that within a couple of years they would all be working for me.

They laughed at my arrogance, telling me there was something wrong and I must have a problem with my head, but I was proved right and I employed each of them at some stage. One became my chauffeur, and was with me for many years before moving to Paris, while his brother still works for me today, and is a very good builder.

This period was cold and wet. It wasn't the best time for seeking construction work, but I got lucky, and was soon offered a job as a labourer on a building site where an extension was being added to the back of a home. It was hard physical work. I had to carry blocks of concrete on my back to the second floor of the scaffolding for as little as £40 a day,but at least I was earning some money and it got me started.

I didn't enjoy the experience, but I had been desperate to get out of the house and earn some money. Because I was already very fit, I was able to work extremely fast. I shocked my bosses when they allocated me three days to carry seven pallets of blocks to the top of the scaffold, and I finished it inside seven hours – although my shoulder was left raw and bleeding at the end of the day.

My next break came very quickly, when I had a call from one of the agencies I'd registered with. I was sent to work for an engineering company who had a site in Oxford Street, the world-famous shopping mecca in the heart of London's West End.

They were part of a major renovation project, and needed someone who knew how to do measurements. Thankfully, just about the only subject I paid any attention to when I was at school was now coming in useful. I joined them straight away, and have never been out of work since that day.

I immediately developed a good relationship with the engineer in Oxford Street, but my English was very poor and I often got muddled. I remember that, one day, when he asked me to get him a coffee, I surprised him when I disappeared for a few minutes and returned holding a shovel!

At the beginning, I remember there were lots of Irish foremen and labourers on the sites. They spoke very loud and fast with a lot of swearing, which made it hard for me to understand what they were saying, especially on the phone.

The only way I could deal with my phone was to turn it off for a few hours at a time as I got on with whichever task I'd been given. But that seemed to make them really crazy. When I turned up at the end of the day to collect my daily sheets, I'd often be met with a torrent of abuse which I'm sure consisted more of expletives than anything else.

At that stage, the Irish were still the dominant manual workforce in London. Contractors knew that, if they sent a van to the corner of Cricklewood Broadway and

Chichele Road first thing in the morning, there would be no shortage of willing workers for hire.

They would point at the ones they wanted, ignore any they knew were blacklisted, and then pack them in the back and head to the site, no questions asked. That began to change as Bulgarians and Romanians arrived in the UK, and we saw the market adapting and shifting.

After a short time living in Neasden Lane, I moved into a nearby house in Braemar Avenue where I shared a room with two new guys. Marius was with the same agency as me and always busy, but Costa never seemed to work and was a complete mystery.

He was also very noisy and had a lot of parties, so I soon packed my bags once again and rented a two-bedroom maisonette just around the corner in Lyndhurst Close. This time I was sharing with four other men, including both my brothers who had recently decided to leave Cârlibaba and come to join me and find work in London – which increased the disappointment of our dad and was yet another example of youth draining away from the village.

My brothers each have very different personalities, and we haven't always been close, partly because I spent a lot of time away from home as a child, and then left the family when I was 18.

Ilie is four years younger than me, which felt like a big gap when we were young. For many years, we didn't get on particularly well as we hardly knew each other and had little in common.

That began to change when I first returned from Portugal. I was surprised and very happy to discover he was suddenly a young man. That made it far easier for us to chat and share things. But he'd also been out of control for a while, and was often out drinking and clubbing and sometimes getting into fights. Vasilie, who was the baby of the family having been born in 1988, was behaving in a very similar way.

It seemed to me as though my dad had perhaps undergone some kind of trauma when I suddenly left without telling him, because he treated them completely differently to the way he had been with me.

As his eldest son, I wasn't allowed to be out after 8pm and was given a lot of restrictions, but these guys were able to get away with murder. They went out drinking and smoking, and stayed out until late with few consequences. Perhaps dad was worn out after a lifetime of struggle, and no longer had the fire left inside.

Ilie decided to accompany me to Portugal when I left Cârlibaba for the second time, and he remained there when I subsequently moved to Paris and then on to London. I had always wanted a brother who was close to me, so we could plan and do things together, but it wasn't that kind of rapport. He was a tough man and an outsider, and it still saddens me that we have always had a slightly distant relationship.

He did, however, help me with a small loan when I moved away from Portugal, while I supported him when he later followed me to London. I even helped him start up his own company, because – despite everything – family bonds are strong, especially for Romanians who grew up in and just after the Ceausescu era.

He later moved back to Romania so we don't see as

much of each other as we used to. Maybe it was inevitable that the sons of Ilie Voloseniuc wouldn't always see eye to eye after the problems of our childhood, but I am very glad we have now become friends as well as brothers.

Vasilie is the troublemaker of the family. The baby and the cheeky one, he has had a few personal issues over the years, but he has a good heart and a kind soul and I always try to look after him. He splits his time between London and Romania, and used to work with me for several years, but I have discovered that being the older brother is definitely an expensive headache at times.

It is a job that we are born into, rather than one we seek. As with so many of the Romanian fairy tales that always seemed to feature three competing brothers, we are very different, but ultimately bonded by the blood of our ancestors.

During those early years in London, we were all living together, and just about tolerating each other without too many arguments. We had a nice house with a small back garden where I could hang my punch-bag on a tree, put up a tent for friends to stay in, and have barbecues in the summer.

Life seemed reasonably calm and happy. I was working hard and, for the first time in my life, managing to save some money for the future when – like the bottle that struck me on the head in Portugal – I was hit hard by another unexpected blow.

It was to become the most stressful experience of my young life. I feared I was going to be made bankrupt, and see all my business dreams and ambitions destroyed, despite being guilty of nothing except naivety.

We rented the house from an agency and, as it was registered in my name, I collected the money from the other four guys and handed over £675 in cash each month to a man called Sam, who always came to collect it himself and gave me a signed receipt. We always paid on time and in full, and never missed a payment.

After we had been happily living there for about ten months, Sam appeared at the house unexpectedly one evening, and asked us to sign a completely new tenancy agreement that stated we had only just moved in. He said something about it being related to an upgrade with the landlord, but as that would have been a lie it didn't seem right. I refused, and told him we were happy with the existing contract.

His mood suddenly changed. He became very agitated and angry, and tried to pressurise me into signing, but when he realised I wasn't going to change my mind he abruptly left. That was the last we ever saw of him.

Shortly afterwards, I was horrified and bewildered when I began receiving threatening legal letters from the landlord, who claimed we owed them £7000 in rent. That was ridiculous, as we had never once missed a payment, so I called the phone number on the form in the hope of quickly clearing up what I thought must have been a misunderstanding.

That was when I discovered I had been scammed by Sam – if that had even been his real name – and that he had regularly taken the money from me but apparently then kept it for himself.

Presumably the landlord had eventually noticed that they owned a property that didn't seem to be bringing in any money, which was why Sam was so insistent that we signed the updated new agreement. It would have suggested that we had only just moved into the house, and he could try to get away with claiming it had previously been sitting empty.

How and why he was able to do that without the landlord realising what he was up to I never did find out. But when I confidently produced the receipts he had given me as proof that we had always paid our rent, I was told they were all fake and that he'd taken advantage of my poor English to make fun of me, signing them as Mr Tea or Mr Coffee or other silly names.

They were worthless and meaningless. I went to the police, but they said there was nothing they could do and I was on my own, even though the situation was clearly outrageously unfair.

It was a terrible period, and very scary as I didn't know what to do. I accidently made things even worse by not engaging a solicitor when the landlord took me to court. It was a stupid decision, as I didn't fully understand what was being said, and couldn't explain what had happened.

Consequently, not only did I lose the case and get ordered to pay the £7000 (which had already been paid in full once), but I was also told to pay the costs of the landlord's legal bill.

They insisted they had no idea who 'Sam' was, but obviously something very strange was going on as no-one ever suggested that we had broken into the property and were illegally squatting. I thought that someone would surely see that we'd been given a contract and were as much a victim of the scam as the landlord, and yet we were now being told we had to pay everything for a second time.

I was in a state of complete shock, as this wasn't what I believed British justice would be. It felt more like the kind of thing that happened in Romania in the bad days. We had paid our rent in full and on time.

The guy had disappeared, the landlord now said they didn't know who he was, and I was in deep trouble without understanding what I had done wrong – other than not yet speaking English to a very good standard.

I told my brothers what had happened, but they just shrugged their shoulders and said it was nothing to do with them. They had given me their rent, and it was my fault I'd lost it. My friend Iacob very generously helped me with some of it, but I was now faced with a huge problem, as the court had given me six weeks to pay it off or be declared bankrupt.

Finally, I found a solicitor, and having gone through all the details he told me I had no available option but to pay up. I knew that bankruptcy would be a total disaster, and wreck any chance I might have of a future business career in England. I decided I had to work as many hours a day as I could, and every day of the week, until the balance was cleared.

Somehow, I managed to do it by taking on every available job. It is one of the things I am most proud of in my life, as it was a monumental achievement and I was exhausted. Despite everything that happened, we actually ended up staying in the house for another couple of years, as we were very happy with it.

The landlords were a big housing association, and I

went to see them at their head office at Charing Cross to discuss what had happened. They realised they should have checked why they weren't getting the rent, and that it reflected very badly on them, so once the arrears had been cleared they were happy for us to remain there and pay them directly.

As life-lessons go, that was a big one that I could have done without. But out of the bad came some good. As well as making me a lot more careful about who I trusted, the experience forced me to focus on learning English as fast as possible.

It wasn't easy as I was always with Romanians at home, and didn't have time to take lessons, but I started listening more closely to people at work, and picked some up by watching TV and listening to the radio.

As with many things in my life, I had to have a reason to make a change. But once my mind was made up, I was able to absorb and learn. An additional bonus was that the solicitor who helped guide me out of that particular mess has become and remains a close friend.

8

Business Beginnings

One afternoon, as we were having a short tea-break while I was doing some agency work, one of the engineers on the site suggested to me that I was good enough to set up my own business – especially as I was passionate about improving things. I thanked him for showing so much confidence in me, but felt that it was way beyond me at that moment.

We carried on with the day's work, and I thought no more of it at that time. But, looking back, I realise that was the first planting of the seed in my mind that was to grow into my first business and the other companies I've subsequently created.

The agency work was uncertain but regular. I was working as a freelance bricklayer, and earning only about £70 a day as I didn't have my own tools, when a friend told me of a potential opportunity to join the crew on a new build that had recently begun in Kentish Town in North-West London. They were offering £150 a day, which was big money for that time. I got in touch, and when I was offered a position with them, I took it straight away.

Unfortunately, this job was to be another test of my character. Even though I was working hard and fulfilling every task, the supervisor took an instant dislike to me. It didn't seem to matter what I did, or how many bricks I laid, it was never right in his eyes, and he'd constantly criticise and shout at me.

It all became too much. Eventually, I had a big falling out with him and decided to start looking for another job. I knew I had to keep going and deal with difficult people and situations, and still felt that almost anything was better than a lifetime spent in a Romanian forest.

But it was a tough period. I had to take a deep breath each morning, look myself in the eyes as I stood in front of the shaving mirror, and tell myself to focus, stay strong and not give up.

I knew I couldn't just walk out, and risk having no income as there were a lot of bills to pay, but I also felt that a drastic change was needed. There was no point in sitting around waiting for something to happen, so I had to give fate a big shove and do something that was way outside my normal comfort zone.

I travelled to Kentish Town each morning, and would go past an office on Leyton Road for a civil engineering company called Mears. When I sometimes stopped in a nearby café for a coffee before work, there were usually Mears staff in there as well, and they always seemed to be happier than the people on the site I was working on.

The next time I was in the café, I took another deep breath, went up to one of the men who was wearing their distinctive jacket, and introduced myself. My English still wasn't very good at that stage, but I think I probably told them I liked their branding and yellow colours, and would be interested in working for them. To my amazement, he suggested I arranged to go and have a chat with them very soon.

I immediately took up the offer, and met with the Mears boss – who was called Bill – just to ensure I had other options available if the next row with my supervisor turned out to be the last. The interview went very well. I felt comfortable and relaxed. At the end of our chat, Bill said he liked me, and gave me his number to call if I ever wanted to have a trial with them, which was a great boost to my confidence.

Even though I despised the supervisor at my current job – especially as his appalling behaviour and mood changes seemed to be directly linked to the drink and drugs he was allegedly taking – the money was very good. I enjoyed the work, and being with the rest of my colleagues, but the situation was having an increasingly negative impact on my mental wellbeing.

Everything came to an inevitable climax a few days later, when, following another massive falling out, I was sacked on the spot. I called in on Bill to explain what had happened, and he was as good as his word, immediately arranging to send me to a site where Mears were the subcontractors.

This new turn in the road of my life was to prove one of the most important. I will forever be grateful for the trust he placed in the young Romanian who turned up at his office that day.

The site was at Tottenham Court Road, in the heart of London's internationally renowned West End theatre and shopping sector, and next to the iconic Centre Point building – a 34 storey tower block that is one of central London's most famous landmarks.

We were working with Balfour Beatty, one of the UK's largest infrastructure and construction companies, who were surveying the area around the existing tube station to see where the services were sited.

The buildings were to be demolished ahead of a major redevelopment, which was part of the Crossrail project to build a new railway line running from east to west under London. It was finally opened in 2022 as the Elizabeth Line.

I started with Mears in September 2007, and, after completing an induction course, was assigned to work as a labourer with a lovely man called Paul Davis. As they didn't know how good I was they said they could only start me on £100 a day. This came as quite a shock, as I hadn't considered that I might be taking a drop in pay.

I wondered whether I'd just made a huge mistake, and if it might have been better to have simply kept my mouth shut at my previous job, but then I thought it could be a good opportunity. I decided I'd stay and give it a go.

Paul was very efficient, and we got on extremely well. He later worked for me as a key team member in one of my businesses, but back then he'd expect me to be at the yard for 6am every morning. We would have a coffee, confirm the day's plans, and get the gear loaded up before driving to the site to start work.

As I was the labourer, and younger and quicker than him, I soon became the main mason. Paul supervised my work, and taught me more about what I was doing. He gave me an opportunity to learn about drainage, paving, driving a dumper, and numerous other aspects of the role. He'd been there many years, and would always take the new staff out with him to train them up, then report back to Bill to let him know if they were any good.

On the downside, being youngest on site meant I also had to do more than my share of the dogsbody work. Yet again, I often found myself making coffees and cleaning the toilets and kitchens, but that was all part of the learning experience, as much as I hated it at the time.

We completed a few other jobs before Christmas, including laying some paving on one of the roads behind Oxford Street. I recall sometimes spotting a man called Mick McLaughlin, who was employed by Bill to go round and check on his teams on the site – a little like the role of a mystery shopper. Fortunately, he told everyone that I was a hard worker, and my contract was automatically extended into the new year. For once, I felt reasonably settled.

Sometimes we'd also work at night, when we had to put out the cones for the traffic management teams. It was very varied, and I saw lots of sides to the business. In addition, this was the first time I was spending each day with English and Irish colleagues. The experience helped my English improve enormously, especially as Paul was teaching that to me as well.

Work seemed to take up all my time during that period. After I'd spent my evenings training in the local gym, I had very little to spare for anything else. I was working in all parts of London, from Croydon to Camden, Bromley to Richmond, so a large part of each day would also be spent travelling. I hardly even had time to join my brothers or our other Romanian friends in the pub.

I stayed with Mears for three months, and enjoyed it a lot. But that little whisper from the engineer was still in the back of my mind, getting ever louder. It prompted me to register myself as self-employed and begin to think more seriously about my future.

When I asked to see Bill to thank him, and explained I was going to leave Mears to set up on my own, he tried to talk me out of it by very kindly offering to pay me a lot more money. But I had already decided that I needed to take a chance and see if I could build my own business. We parted on very good terms, but I also had to face a new reality: I was out of work, and had no income.

Having previously mainly carried out agency work as a labourer, I was fully aware that I was now starting back at the bottom of the building and civil engineering food chain. But I was also confident that all would come good, because I was always watching and seeing how I thought things could be improved. I was excited about generating my own opportunities to put my many ideas into practice – this time as my own boss.

Fortunately, I had a fierce and instinctive drive and passion. That is something that hasn't changed, as one of my biggest motivations is still to see how we can innovate and make work conditions better for my teams, deliver our contracts quicker and ever more efficiently to our clients, while also doing our best to protect and improve the neighbourhoods and environment we are working in.

I decided to go home to Romania to spend Christmas with my family in December 2007. I was enjoying a relatively stress-free few days when, just a couple of days into the new year, Bill surprised me by leaving me a voicemail that said '*Hello Stefan, happy new year, I hope you are well. You said you were going to take on your own jobs and I have one going at Westfield in Shepherd's Bush, do you want to take it on?*'

I was astonished, but very excited, that a contract was available at the enormous new Westfield Shopping Centre complex that was being built at White City in West London, opposite the legendary BBC Television Centre.

The main project was apparently running a long way behind schedule, but still due to finally open in October 2008, so there were plenty of jobs available as all the contractors rushed to hit their deadlines.

I responded straight away to let Bill know that I would definitely like to accept. I said I would be available to start with an experienced drainage team in less than a week, although I'm not sure I told him I was actually in Romania!

I was staying with my sister Ana Maria at her home in Oradea at this point. Initially, I had no idea how I would either be able to actually do the job, or who I could employ to work on it with me. At that stage, I had no team, but I decided this was too good an opportunity to miss. I felt sure that somehow I would make it work. Here was an unexpected stepping stone into the world of business.

I'd driven from London in the three-year old Audi A4 I'd bought on finance, but as I didn't have enough money to purchase new tyres, I was on second-hand ones. This meant I had to be very careful in the snow when I braked as we drove through the mountain regions.

Vasilie and Ilie had come with me, as well as a woman from Cârlibaba who lived in London. The journey out was a lovely experience and took about 30 hours as we meandered the 1300 miles through France, Belgium, Germany, Austria and Hungary to reach our parents' home.

I had planned to take another relaxing couple of days on the return leg, but following Bill's messages I packed up and left almost immediately to drive straight back to London on my own.

My priorities were to urgently recruit a team, and to get hold of some tools. I was determined to show Bill that I was capable of doing the job. I knew it was vitally important I made a good impression, as this could be an invaluable opportunity.

Once I was back in London, I started making calls to all the people I knew who had experience in working on drainage projects. To encourage them to come on board straight away, I offered some extremely good rates.

In fact, I offered so much money that we didn't earn enough to pay everyone at first. I had to dip into my own savings to ensure everything went smoothly, but that was probably one of the best decisions of my career.

I arranged for a big guy called Adrian to be the main mason who would lay the drains. He must have been happy with how it all went, as he later worked with me for many years. I also needed a labourer and tracked down a guy called Tibi. He was a very skinny man I had heard was looking for work, and fortunately the pair of them were ready and available to attend the induction session that Mears always ran.

They were a very odd couple to look at. Adrian was probably 120kg to Tibi's 60, so they resembled Laurel and Hardy. But, fortunately for me, with better results and far less drama.

I'd first met Tibi in strange circumstances during the previous year, when I helped a Romanian I knew as Fericire. He would make regular trips between London and Romania in his minibus to bring back packages and labourers (all completely legally). We'd sometimes let him sleep in a tent in our back garden, as he was a nice guy and was no trouble at all.

One day in the spring of 2007, Fericire asked to speak with me. I could see he was looking very concerned, which was unusual as he was normally so relaxed. He explained that he had three men who were coming in from Romania that day, but had been let down by the agent who had arranged their accommodation.

He'd taken their money and had now vanished, and was refusing to answer their increasingly concerned calls or texts. The three young guys were now in danger of being left on the street.

Having had my own painful experience of someone absconding with my rent, I felt bad for them. I told Fericire to bring them to my house, and I'd see what I could do to help. Tibi, Alex and Ion all seemed to be decent people when we met and had a chat, so I gave them a tent to stay in for a few days in our garden while I helped find them rooms in nearby Neasden.

They later told me they were very anxious and in a bit

of a panic about this strange man with a Russian name and lots of muscles who had a boxing punch-bag hanging from the tree next to their tent. They didn't understand why he would help them for free.

Apparently, they managed to talk themselves into such a state that they even came up with a plan to stay alert and on their guard at night, so they could be ready to fight if my brothers and I tried to attack them in the dark.

They were genuinely scared we'd steal and sell their organs, as there were a lot of rumours being spread back home that healthy young Romanians were being targeted for that when they travelled to London. Fake news is clearly not a new phenomenon.

I'm happy to say that the three of them finally relaxed after I helped them find accommodation, and introduced them to some agencies who fixed them up with jobs. When I came back in January, I gave them a call to see if any were free, and as Tibi was between jobs, he joined us straight away.

After the induction we were allocated an Irish supervisor called Jonathan, and set to work on the job. Jonathan was very funny, but regularly left me messages that I struggled to understand as he had such a strong accent. Sometimes he'd complain that we didn't have the right tools, but the truth was that I only owned a single trowel, and everything else was being borrowed as and when we needed it.

I was very strict with Adrian and Tibi, and told them that they had to look after that trowel unless they wanted a big problem as it was my entire tool kit. Unfortunately, they just laughed because it was so rusty. But it was also very symbolic, as it was the tool that enabled me to start my journey.

We worked hard and did a good job and Mears were very happy. But when the time came for us to get paid, I was shocked to discover they didn't just hand out bundles of notes as most of my previous bosses had done. It might seem surprising that I was so naïve, even at that stage, but everyone I'd worked with until that point had either paid cash or, more recently, automatically credited my wages straight into my bank account as I was an employee.

Instead, I was now told that as I was self-employed, I'd have to submit a valuation and then raise an invoice. As I had no idea what that was and had never seen one, Bill patiently explained exactly how I had to write down what the job was, where and when it had taken place, what the guys had done, how much time it had taken, and how much we had agreed for the fee. He said I would have to send him the invoice before he could pay us the money.

He also provided me with a template, but as I didn't have anything to actually write it on, I took it to a lady I knew from one of the agencies. She agreed to create the invoice, but charged me something like four per cent as a commission.

With that extra outgoing, and the fact that I'd promised Adrian and Tibi above average pay for the job, I didn't have anything left for myself. But we'd performed well enough to keep Bill contracting us for other work on the project.

I was able to start saving some money from those jobs, and, along with the income from some additional work I was doing on my own, I finally bought a laptop, and spent a night learning how to calculate and write a valuation and raise an invoice myself.

It took several hours, and a lot of frustrated shouting at the screen, but eventually it was finished. I proudly delivered it to Bill with a great sense of satisfaction that I'd now made the switch. From being just another labourer for hire, I'd graduated to the status of an independent businessman.

Gradually, the new way of working began to stabilise. Mears were providing me with an increasing number of jobs, and I managed to renegotiate the rates I was paying the men. After I explained why they were getting more than I could afford, they understood the situation. They were fine with everything, as they enjoyed working with me, and also admitted they'd thought it was too good to be true.

In February 2008, we were also carrying out some work for a very difficult Romanian called Chris, doing a series of jobs on driveways and walls. One day, we had a big falling out. (As you will have realised by now, there are a lot of arguments within the construction and road-building community!) So I started walking around North London looking for possible opportunities, visiting different sites, talking to people and asking if anyone had work.

When I spotted an Irish team employed on the traffic lights at a main junction, I went over and asked if they needed any gangs or masons to build their chambers. It was great timing, as they were just about to recruit staff for those roles. They gave me the number of their boss, a lovely man called Pat. I called him, and we met up to discuss what he needed.

They had a contract with Transport For London (TFL) to upgrade traffic lights, which included a need for brick and concrete junction boxes to hold the cabling. Pat was happy to try us out, but on the strict condition that we provided our own vans and tools. I assured him that wasn't a problem, and we shook hands on a price-work agreement, which meant doing the job for an agreed overall fee rather than getting paid an hourly rate.

I left his office knowing this was another great chance for us to expand our experience and reputations, but also aware that I had two rather major problems. The first was that I didn't have any vans. The second was that I didn't have any tools, just my trusty trowel and a new laptop for writing invoices.

It was a potentially large complication, for all the obvious reasons, and the only solution I could see would need me to take a deep breath, swallow my pride, and ask Chris for a very large favour, while hoping he'd forgotten all the names I'd called him just a few days previously.

I knew he had a lot of vans in his yard, and that they weren't all being used. So I gave him a call, and very politely asked if I could possibly borrow one for a few days if I covered the fuel costs. To my surprise, he didn't seem to be harbouring any grudges, and immediately agreed.

I took a bus to Wembley, collected the van, and drove it back to my home in Neasden where we had our entire tool collection – which now consisted of a rusty old wheelbarrow and a few shovels that were lying in the garden.

I'd recently taken on a new labourer, another Romanian called Eugen, and after loading the van we got out our copy of the famous and essential road map of London: the

A-Z. We looked up the address of the work, and set off back towards Wembley again.

We discovered, to our horror, that the job was quite literally outside the entrance to Chris's yard. We'd just driven a giant loop and arrived back where we had started.

I couldn't believe our bad luck, and was very embarrassed and concerned as I knew Chris would not be impressed if he saw us there. Not unnaturally, he would want to know if we were playing a game with him. Why had we asked to borrow a van and then parked it right outside his own doorstep?

Just as we started to check the address we'd been given by Pat, we spotted the rest of the TFL team by the junction. It was 11am, and we needed to unload and get going on the job. But, inevitably, just as I was looking around for somewhere to hide the van, Chris came storming out of his office gesticulating and angrily shouting '*Stefan what are you doing? What the fuck did you need the van for?!*'

I tried to be very laid-back and detached. I told him that I had another job elsewhere, but had just come back for a short period to help the rest of my team with a problem they were having with the junction. Unfortunately, that failed to convince him. Completely losing his temper, he demanded I returned the van immediately.

I started to panic. I could sense there was a very real danger that the whole thing was about to fall apart. I felt like a juggler who has thrown his balls too far in the air, and isn't sure exactly where they are going to come down. But I managed to calm him, and get him to agree that I'd bring the van back at the end of the week.

Once that minor crisis was out of the way, we worked

extremely hard for three long days, as we were new to this firm and wanted to impress Pat and his colleagues. My guys left at 3pm, but I stayed until at least 5pm. Then, on one of the evenings, I noticed that my new boss had set a test for me that could have been a trap if I'd had a different type of character.

When Pat's team finished for the day, they 'accidentally' left an expensive petrol saw on the site. I put it safely in my van overnight, and told them I'd kept it for them when we all met again on the following morning. Having passed the trial, Pat came to see me on the Wednesday afternoon to say how pleased he was with our work.

As I was feeling guilty about deceiving such a decent man, and was sure I'd be found out soon anyway, I decided to be honest. I told him I'd only borrowed the van as I really wanted to get the job, but now the guy wanted it back. I followed that up by asking if there was any chance that he could lend me a van himself?

There was a slight pause as Pat took in what I said. But, to my enormous relief, he assured me that it wouldn't be a problem – although I thought he left the room with an enigmatic half-smile as he clapped his hand across my shoulder and said he'd sort it out for me.

Pat certainly did that, and on the Friday morning our replacement van arrived, although it was not exactly what we'd hoped for or expected. Waiting for us, and tucked away in a far corner at the site, was a truly horrible, dirty, bad smelling, nasty pile of rust with filthy windows, full of rubbish and rat droppings. He'd been true to his word and provided us with a van. The nightmare van.

Whereas Chris had lent us a white 1997 Ford Transit

box van, Pat had provided a very old yellow LDV where all the weight training I'd been doing in the evenings came in useful as I had to crank the steering halfway round before the wheels even began to turn.

I told the guys that we had to look on it as a blessing. At least we now had our own transport to take us to jobs in all parts of London where there were junctions that needed building. That weekend we set about cleaning the van, and gradually brought it back to life.

It took us quite a few hours. But once it had been well and truly scrubbed, it no longer looked as though it was in danger of being towed away for scrap. Plus, as the van was already insured as part of Pat's fleet contract, that was another crucial expense we'd saved.

At the end of that first week's work, Pat gave me a cheque to cover the team's pay. I was in a state of shock as it came to just over £2000 more than anything we'd ever earned before. That was the start of a very happy, trusting and profitable relationship with Pat. He asked me to provide him and his projects with an increasing number of teams. By the end of the year, we had many men working on sites all around London.

Somehow, I had accidently found myself working as a one-man recruitment agency. But, rather than sitting in an office, I had the added benefit that I still worked on the sites myself every day. As a result, I was able to stay across the men and the work, which led to a strong bond of trust. Pat paid me, I paid the men, and everyone was happy. 2008 was a very good year for me, as I grew from employing two men to having a team of many dozens on my books.

On top of that, Bill came back with more jobs for

Mears. As our reputation for quality, delivery and value for money began to spread, we were approached by other companies who wanted us to work with them. I signed a wide variety of contracts. As well as the TFL and Crossrail sites, we were working on houses, laying driveways, building walls, landscaping, and delivering many other projects.

Pat was a truly amazing mentor and support. Later that year, he kindly lent me vans for other jobs as well, even when I was working on projects for Mears. He became a very close and trusted friend. He also lent me money and tools to help me build my business, and gave me so much advice. Pat was one of the first people I invited to our wedding.

He was from Ireland, but had come to England as a young man, and must have been about 41 when I first met him. Unfortunately, he also had a crazy side to his character, and enjoyed a very lively social life away from work. Nothing prepared me for the call I took that informed me he'd died of a sudden heart attack when he was only 45. I was devastated as he was like an older brother to me, and I still miss him to this day.

9

Simona

I met my wife Simona by mistake. But it was a mistake that changed my life for ever, and is the reason why I have beautiful children playing in the house as I sit at home in Wembley and write these words.

In this modern world, there are many different ways that people can meet their soulmate. Some are introduced by family or friends. Others meet in bars, clubs or workplaces. And, of course, many now connect through dating apps and websites.

My way, however, was slightly different. Rather than swiping right, it was the result of a sim-card mix-up on a mobile phone in a queue for a Romanian car wash! Not very romantic in itself perhaps, but it led to the romance of my life.

In July 2008, all was going well in London. I was

happily settling into my routine in the city, gradually picking up the language, and living with my brothers in a house we rented in Edgware. I had plenty of work, and was beginning to save some money, while thinking about how I could develop my own business and plan for the future.

Life was good, although a seemingly very nice and developing relationship with a woman I'd met at church in Holborn had ended abruptly, when I discovered she was still seeing her former boyfriend behind my back. Unsurprisingly, I wasn't very happy with that arrangement. So, as a consequence, I was a single man again when I decided to fly back home to Romania to visit my family that month.

It was especially lovely to see my mum, and catch up about everything that had been going on in the village, while also telling her about all I'd been doing in London. By this stage, my dad had grudgingly accepted that I'd made my home in England, so he was slightly easier to talk with as we walked in the hills and forests of Cârlibaba.

It was also re-energising to get some fresh mountain air into my lungs after many months of living and working near the heavily polluted – and almost permanently static – North Circular Road in London.

There was a local girl called Simona I'd known when I was younger, and as I was going to be in the area for a few days, I thought I'd look her up and see if she'd like to meet for a drink. The opportunity to contact her came one morning when I took my hire car to be washed. As there was the inevitable long queue, I scrolled through my phone to find her number.

I thought I'd surprise her with a call, but when she answered, I was the one who was very puzzled. Her voice sounded so different to the way I remembered. I asked what her name was, and she became very indignant and told me that I was being extremely rude. I ought to know, she said, as I was the one who had just called her – especially as I was always telling her how much I loved her voice!

I wasn't quite sure how to reply, so there was a very awkward pause before she asked if it was Sil who was calling. When I replied '*No, I'm Stefan,*' she laughed and said that Sil's number had shown up on her phone. That was when I realised my mistake. When I'd borrowed my brother Vasilie's mobile as I left the house, I'd forgotten to switch it to my sim card. I had actually dialled a different and younger Simona, who was a good friend of his.

This one must be Simona Juravle, I thought. A girl who I remembered having an amazing figure when we'd briefly met the previous Christmas, for the first time in many years. So I immediately asked if she'd like to get together and have a tea or coffee before I went back to London.

She said she'd be happy to, and would send me a text letting me know when and where to meet. With that slightly loose arrangement, the brief and somewhat awkward conversation came to an end.

The car finally got its clean, and as I drove to my childhood home, I thought back to the time when the young Simona had first come into our lives. It happened in 1991, when I was just a small child of eight. She'd been born on March 5, 1989, to Parasca and Radu. She was christened Georgeta Simona Juravle, but was always known by her middle name.

Tragically, her father suddenly died of leukaemia not long after her second birthday, and the whole village was shocked at the terrible loss – especially as Parasca was left with four young children.

I have a very clear memory of my grandparents going to Radu's funeral, and then coming back home and quietly sharing their concerns about what was to become of the family. They were worried about how the Juravle family would be able to live, as it was a period of so many shortages and restrictions.

I will never forget sitting under the kitchen table, playing with my toy tractors, and hearing them sadly talking about the poor little girl who would never remember her dad. I suddenly had a strong and intense feeling inside me that she needed looking after and protecting.

I pleaded with my parents and grandparents to let her come and live with us, so we could feed and care for her, but they gave me a hug and explained why that would not be possible or practical. Our lives all moved on and found their own individual paths.

Seventeen years later, I thought about Simona again. I felt that perhaps that feeling had always been there, and had never really left me. I wondered if the accidental contact had been God-given, and was meant to be.

If God was indeed involved in our reconnection, he certainly wasn't in a hurry to move things along. I heard nothing else from Simona, and assumed she'd only agreed to meet as a way of swiftly ending a strange and unexpected phone call.

By the night I was due to fly back to London, I'd given up all hope of meeting up. I was finishing my packing at home with the assistance of mum, and talking about some refurbishment work I was going to help her with, when I heard my phone ping.

It was a text from Simona apologising for not having been in touch as she'd been very busy, but wishing me luck and suggesting that maybe we could meet up again in the future when I was back in Romania.

I have always been quite shy around women, and hadn't wanted to contact her in the previous week as I was afraid I'd seem too brash or rude. But this was definitely a small opening, and I was determined not to waste the unexpected opportunity.

I immediately replied to say that I still had a couple of hours before leaving for the airport, and would love to see her before I went if she was free. To my surprise, she came around straight away for a quick chat.

That was when the magical connection began. It seemed as though we had been friends for ever. Even in that brief time, it just felt natural and comfortable to be together. When I was back in London, we kept in touch on the phone and were soon speaking every day, often several times a day, as we discovered we shared so many ambitions and aspirations.

While I was working on the various sites, I couldn't get her out of my thoughts. I was so impatient to see Simona again that at the end of August I went back home to Romania for a fortnight. I wanted to see if our feelings were as strong when we were together as they were when we spoke on the phone each day.

We spent many happy hours during those two weeks, and, even though things were already moving very quickly,

I was fast coming to a decision about how I hoped our future would develop.

After a few more weeks back working in London, I once again flew into Cluj airport in Transylvania. As I drove to Cârlibaba in my hire car, I thought through my feelings and hopes and plans. I had grown up in a post-revolutionary country that was so unstable and uncertain that I had become someone who believed in taking fast decisions. My generation didn't know what problems a delay could bring.

Simona had just finished her first year studying public relations at St Stefan University in Suceava. She was about to return for the second year when I made a suggestion that took her completely by surprise, and changed both of our lives forever.

One evening, as we sat by the Cârlibaba river looking across at the forests where our fathers had worked, I explained that although I really cared for her, I was looking for more than a long-distance phone relationship.

I already instinctively knew she was the soulmate I wanted to share my life with. So I asked her to return to London with me, to begin a life together in a country that offered us many more opportunities than we could ever find at home.

I also explained that I would completely understand if that seemed to be an utterly ridiculous suggestion. I said that if she wanted to remain at university to complete her degree we could still be friends, and I'd help her wherever possible, but I was looking for a partner to settle down and start a family with. I hoped it would be her.

Not surprisingly, Simona was pretty shocked at the

suggestion of such a massive leap forward into a new level of our relationship. I can scarcely believe I had the nerve to ask her that, after dating each other for just a couple of months – and with most of our conversations taking place on the phone.

Looking back now, I realise what a massive risk it was for her. I was fine. I had a home and work and friends, and was beginning to pick up the language. But she was based in Cârlibaba with her uncle, while her mother, step-father, four siblings and friends all lived locally, so it was a huge change for her to make. When she said yes, I definitely thanked God that night, and was as happy as I have ever been in my life.

Family history was inadvertently repeating, and the unexpected news didn't go down well with everyone. Her uncle was furious, and insisted she stay there and finish her studies. Her friends told her she was crazy, that she hardly knew me.

But Simona is a strong-willed woman who, like me, knows her own mind. Because something inside her said this was the right thing to do, she agreed. She told me that she trusted me.

At the age of 19, she gave up her university, family, friends and life in Romania to move to North London and live with a man she'd only really known for a few months.

Even as I was celebrating the news, I was fully aware of the need to be realistic and give some thought to the practical arrangements I'd need to make at home. At that time, I sublet the spare bedrooms in the house to my two brothers, so my first task was to ask them to leave and find new homes.

It wasn't the easiest of conversations, but fortunately they understood the situation, and saw I was in love. They immediately moved out together into a nearby property. This meant Simona and I had some space when she arrived. We were able to start getting to know each other properly and with some privacy. Something that hadn't exactly been easy in a small Romanian village.

As you will have realised by now, once I make my mind up about doing something, I can never see the point of delaying. Whether in my personal life or in business, the approach is the same for me. Time is precious, and once lost can never be recovered, so we should never waste it.

Now that we were living together in London, the next obvious step was to get married. I proposed during a brief trip to Paris and, once again, Simona said yes. We'd already decided that we wanted to start a family together. Even though we were both still young, I wanted the chance to be a good father.

We had both come from unstable family backgrounds. Simona's father had died before she had the opportunity to know him, and her mother had remarried. As I've already discussed, my upbringing was very complicated, since I didn't get on with my own father and regularly spent long periods staying away from home as a child.

I'm sure that played a big part in the speed of our decisions. We both wanted a real home, where we could bring up our children in a safe, secure and loving environment. I was driven by a deep need to provide for my wife and family, and make sure they didn't suffer from the hunger and fear of poverty that I grew up with.

My British friends are still astonished when they learn there was a place in Europe where life was so troubled during a time as recent as the 1980s and 1990s – a time when they were partying and studying, Margaret Thatcher and Tony Blair were revolutionising the way the country was run, and new technology was driving so many changes to Britain and improving lifestyles for the majority.

I do not wish to disrespect anyone in the UK who struggled with their own jobs and incomes during that period, but the poorest areas in Britain were still vastly better off and more comfortable than huge swathes of post-Ceausescu Romania, especially in the villages where we still had horses and carts when I was a child.

I understood what it was like to grow up in a place where food was often a luxury. My children were not going to experience that level of poverty, and I was anxious to meet them as soon as possible.

Once again, the arrangements had to be made very quickly. But I still wanted us to have a special wedding that would show our family and friends that we were serious about our love. This was a union we wanted to be blessed by God as well as the law.

We got married on October 11, 2008, in the beautiful and historic 300-year-old St Mary le Strand church in London. Although this is an Anglican church, it has also embraced the growing Romanian community in the area, and many now worship there.

This stunning building, a short walk from such iconic landmarks as St Paul's Cathedral and the Old Bailey court, could not have made for a greater contrast to our home village. I was so proud we were able to say our vows there.

My parents were supportive of our marriage – although, when you consider that they had also wed within three months of meeting, they were hardly in a position to criticise us for moving so rapidly. I arranged for them to fly over, along with Simona's mum and aunt, and we had a large number of guests who joined us for the service.

Sadly, some of her closest friends refused to come to London, as they were still trying to convince her she was making a terrible decision. So her bridesmaids were new friends that she'd made in London: Anca and Tibi's girlfriend Gabriella.

Simona chose the wedding dress from a local boutique in Enfield, and we found our ring in a nearby jewellers. I was in serious danger of becoming described as a romantic, albeit one who didn't like to wait!

Ion Sima and George Costea were my joint best men. George was better known as Skinny George, for obvious reasons. Having worked with him when I first arrived in the UK, we became great friends, and he now works with us. Ion was another close and trusted friend I'd lived with in London.

My only suit had a rare outing, and I wore a blue shirt and tie. That's a colour that has followed me around all my life. It is especially relevant now, as blue is the colour of many of my business logos, part of the Romanian flag and the Union Flag and also associated with the Conservative Party in England. I have been a member and supporter of the party for several years, and am very proud to be honorary president of the Conservative Friends of Romania.

After the service, we had our formal sit-down reception and wedding cake in the upstairs room of an

Indian restaurant in Hendon called Raw Spice, close to the local reservoir. Until that year it had been a famous local pub called the Upper Welsh Harp that we'd visited a few times. It was an ideal location for our guests, who were an eclectic mix of Romanian, British, Asian and Irish.

I'd booked a Romanian folk-music group, and they helped round off a fantastic and multicultural event in fairly riotous fashion, with a lot of drinking and dancing that led to many sore heads and legs the following day.

Skinny George was also nursing sore pride as he had offered to drive some of the guests home in his prized BMW 320 M Sports. He has always denied it, but I think he was showing off his car when he misjudged a bend and went straight into a tree. Fortunately, they were all unhurt and were saved by the airbags, but the car was a wreck.

As it turned out, the wedding was the easy bit of our whirlwind relationship. For the first few weeks and months, married life was a lot tougher than either of us had expected, especially as we had such different backgrounds and experiences. The car-crash metaphor was certainly appropriate, and there were occasions when airbags would have been useful!

It was extremely challenging at times, as we faced the reality that we actually hardly knew each other. And yet, there we were in our bedroom, facing the fact we were going to be together for the whole of our lives.

There were occasions when that seemed like a very long life sentence. We had so many huge arguments in the first few months that, if Simona had owned a place to return to in Romania, I'd probably have suggested she went. I would even have bought her the ticket. And I know that she would have happily done the same for me at times.

But, as with most couples, we worked on our differences, celebrated what we had in common, and managed to overcome our problems. One of the things that kept me going was the knowledge that Simona had nowhere else to go, and I had to look after her. We just about survived a torrid first trip back to Romania at Christmas, but managed to get through the storms, and gradually settled into a wonderful life with each other.

That initial attraction steadily grew into a deep and lasting loving relationship. As our children arrived in the next few years, we found ourselves with the family unit we'd both so strongly desired.

The strange thing is that, having moved away from Cârlibaba at such a young age, I ended up as the only one of our five siblings who married a local girl from our own village. My mum and dad loved that their wayward son had finally shown himself to be a conservative traditionalist at heart.

When we tell people that we'd got married after only really knowing each other for three months, they think we were crazy. But I make my mind up very fast. Sometimes in life that approach works out, and sometimes it doesn't.

Fortunately, our marriage did. I often think back to the moment when I sat under a table as a small child, listening to my grandparents talking about the young Simona, and wonder if perhaps it was always meant to be.

10

My First Business

One of the many bonuses of marrying Simona was that I now not only had a life partner, but also a business one. It was so good to have someone else I could discuss projects and contracts with, and from the very beginning she took on key roles as we decided to make some big changes and advances.

It was a specific set of circumstances that prompted us to create our first business. Towards the end of 2009, we'd heard there was an important contract coming up to replace the traffic lights in front of Buckingham Palace, the home of Her Majesty the Queen.

Because the contractor who was overseeing the works would only employ a limited company, we took the decision to set up as such. Fortunately, we were successful in our pitch, and that change took us to a new level of business and professionalism.

I had built up an extensive network across the industry. Now, with an increasing number of contracts becoming available, it also just seemed to be the right time to take another step forward. On September 20, 2009, I registered our first limited company.

It was an enormously proud moment. I was excited about beginning the next stage of the journey of a penniless teenager who had left a small village in Northern Romania.

In reality, it was just a legal formality, as I'd already been working in a self-employed capacity for a long time. This was mainly a case of changing the paperwork. But I was also excited about the prospect of working in front of the Palace for eight months. We were there from just before Christmas until the following summer.

As part of the contact, we worked on several junctions in front of the Palace. Then we moved on to others along The Mall, around Trafalgar Square, down Whitehall and even in Downing Street, outside the homes of the British prime minister and the chancellor of the exchequer. Our main work involved installing traffic light upgrades with new junction boxes, renewing the crossing points, and removing all the parts that were out of date.

Fortunately, the team did a superb job and the feedback was excellent. Shortly after the initial contract was completed, we were awarded another major batch of replacement work that went from Victoria Station to Vauxhall Bridge and across the Thames to a point in front of the MI6 Building. As fans of James Bond will be aware, that is the home of the Secret Intelligence Service – the UK's foreign intelligence agency.

My friends and family found it very funny that a Romanian with a Ukranian name was laying cables right underneath MI6, but we assumed they had checked us out as we were there for almost nine months. One strange thing was that I began to notice pop-up adverts for MI6 and foreign office recruitment appearing alongside my web searches. I sometimes wondered if I was being watched and stalked online.

Before starting on the projects, we had to fill in a lot of special documents, while all our workers were individually vetted by the Palace and MI6. It was very strict, and the police would always check under all our cones as well.

Almost everyone was approved, but I do remember an Iranian guy who came for an interview with us when we were recruiting for those jobs. He took the tests, but the police turned down his paperwork, and we never saw him again.

The police were always friendly, but they did seem very alert, and the whole area around MI6 is also covered by a vast network of cameras. I saw them in action one morning when I was parked in my usual space by the river, outside a coffee shop I visited each day.

As the police had come to know me across the previous months, I'd never had any problems. But on this particular day, a new supervisor for one of the other contractors spotted where I had pulled into, and thought he'd park alongside me.

Unfortunately for him, he was under a different contract, and his name hadn't been passed for security clearance. He had only just stopped, and was getting out of his car, when armed police appeared from all sides, surrounded the vehicle and demanded to know his details and what he was doing there. It was a very impressive display as their response was instant. He rapidly explained, apologised, and drove away.

As I write this in 2023, we now have offices in many locations including in Bucharest, Cluj, Oxfordshire and our main base on a large site in Borehamwood in Hertfordshire, just north of London. It is close to the world-famous Elstree TV and film studios where many iconic BBC productions have been recorded. Not to mention numerous globally successful films, including the Star Wars, James Bond and Indiana Jones franchises.

Back in 2009, however, things were very different. At first, it was just me and Simona working from the small home we were living in on Homefield Road, Edgware. We kept our tools in a shed in our garden, and parked the vans wherever we could find space.

Pat had yet again been a guardian angel, lending us some vans for a few months as well as selling us one of his older ones. I had two teams working on the Buckingham Palace project, and we had other teams doing paving and maintenance work in Camden.

At the same time, we also won a good contract in Baldock town centre in Hertfordshire, north of London, that involved a lot of work, including paving. After that, we developed an important relationship with another major construction company, Skanska, and we've steadily built up our business from there.

As ever, we were acutely aware of the dangers we faced from outside influences that were beyond our control.

Britain, like so much of the world, was still in the early stages of dealing with the great financial crash of 2008-09 – the worst to hit the global finance markets for 80 years. There was a lot of uncertainty as budgets were slashed, and leading institutions crumbled.

For that reason, we took the decision not to hire anyone else as full-time staff, but instead to rely on a wide network of self-employed workers. A number of them are still with me, more than a dozen years later.

The biggest change I noticed was in my drastically increased workload, as the new business gave me more responsibility, and produced a lot more paperwork. Building the company was a full-time responsibility. We regularly worked late into the night, and across the weekends and holiday periods.

As a result, I rarely ventured into Soho or any of the extraordinarily varied and historic tourist places London has to offer. All those galleries, theatres and museums might as well have been on the other side of the planet, as there was no chance I would have the time to explore them.

That's something I really hope can change for my children. This is one of the greatest cities in history, with such an incredible range and diversity of experiences available. I think it is as important that they see and learn about those as it is that they stay close to their Romanian heritage as well.

Another person who really made a difference when I set up the company – and was faced with the problems of dealing with increasingly complex contracts – was Miraj Shah. He was the trainee solicitor I alluded to earlier, when

I had the issue with the rented house where the mysterious Sam vanished with the rent I'd handed over each month.

I met Miraj when I went to Shah Solicitors in Braemar Avenue on Neasden Lane to ask for their advice. My English was very poor, and having just lost the court case, I was angry and confused about what to do.

It was Miraj who convinced me that, even though I had been the victim of a massive scam, it was best to pay it all back. If I was made bankrupt, that would create many long-term problems. I'm glad to say I took his advice. With his help and wisdom, I managed to get through that horrible period. We subsequently became such close friends that I regard him almost as a member of my family.

Shortly after that first episode, he told me he had a garage at his home that needed some work doing on it, and asked for an estimate. As I already thought he was a very nice person, I offered to do it for cost if he could help me with my paperwork in return. I was just starting out, and didn't understand a lot of the documents I was being asked to sign by my various different employers.

We were both happy with that arrangement, so I bought the materials and worked at his house during the evenings and on weekends. Since that time, whenever I've had a contract I'm not sure about, or a client who hasn't paid up on time, Miraj will write the legal letters on my behalf. Having a trusted friend and solicitor on my side was one of the best things that could have happened to me.

We also used to go clubbing and drinking together when we were younger, although I suspect those days are now behind us. But I'd do anything for him, and am very grateful we met – even it if did come about because I was being ripped off at the time. Proof, yet again, that good things can come out of bad experiences.

As I've been looking back through my life as part of the research for this book, it has repeatedly struck me how often I've been so lucky to have key people around me when I needed them.

Launching my own business sounds so easy when I see it written down all these years later. But at the time it was a scary experience, as well as an exciting one. When we were first setting up, I spoke to a lot of people who had their own businesses to ask for advice, and even begged some of them to join me as a partner in the new company, but they all said no.

On reflection, I'm glad that we had to learn to do everything on our own. One irony is that almost everyone I approached would later work for me as a subcontractor on one of my projects.

Simona was pregnant with Sofia-Maria when our first business was founded. Our first child arrived in our life in November 2009. I was out on the sites every day, but fortunately Simona was able to continue to work from home and look after Sofia-Maria at the same time. She took on responsibility for recruitment, as we looked to grow our staff and sign new contracts.

We didn't have a website or anything like that until about 2014 or 2015. We mainly found our staff via word of mouth or personal reference – although we did also initially place adverts on a few websites such as 'Romanians in the UK'" and mainly ended up employing Romanian workers at that time.

It just happened that way, as we all spoke the same language, and they were the ones we were put in touch with. Simona would speak to the applicants and create a shortlist of people for me to interview and test. The system worked very well.

In those early days, we were mainly a labour supplier. But then, from 2010 and 2011, we started to take jobs that required us to also provide materials and plant. This required further expansion and new skills. I remember the first time I accepted a job to supply and fit out a project, and realised that we had no idea how to get the concrete.

We had to open up accounts with the concrete plant and tarmac suppliers. It was another big commitment, and a difficult step at first, but we built as we went on. We had no choice but to rapidly learn to understand every single aspect of running a company.

Throughout that period, I was still doing the physical work myself. I was on a site almost every day, digging, cleaning, building and being a very active part of the teams. As the business grew, we started purchasing storage facilities for the materials and containers and plant and tools, so my working days started earlier and finished later.

I used to be at the petrol station at 5am to fill up the cans of petrol we'd need that day, and sort out the right tools for each job. That way, the men would just have to come to the yard and they would be able to collect everything.

I'd also give them instructions and notes on what was required. After they left the yard to get started on the project, I'd go to visit the clients and discuss what they wanted. Then I would return to the site to check the quality and see that the men were working properly, before sending out the invoices, doing the accounts, and paying the wages.

I did this for at least a couple of years, until we could finally afford a secretary. Then we took on a storeman and a mechanic and a yardman. This was how I built the company up. I probably worked on the jobs myself until about 2015, which was when I was able to take a more managerial role.

But it has meant that I can look everyone who works for me in the eye. I can tell them that I know exactly what their job requires, and that they need to do it as I've done it myself.

The birth of Sofia-Maria was the most emotionally moving time of my life. I always thought that I wanted a boy, and even when Simona had her first scan in Barnet Hospital and the nurse told us we were having a daughter, I was convinced they must be wrong and that it was bound to be a boy.

Those final few weeks of pregnancy were a magical period. I remember how we would go to the park together, and as we sat on a bench I would put my hand on the bump and feel the baby moving under my hand.

It was unlike anything I had ever experienced before. I know that my whole being changed with the realisation that our family of two was about to become three, as we would have this tiny person to look after.

Simona's aunt Domnica very kindly came from Romania to help support her, as I was working throughout that whole period. But we were both at Barnet Hospital with her when she went into labour.

My poor wife looked exhausted, and was breathing with the help of an oxygen mask. When she kept asking me if I could see anything, I felt I should be encouraging and tell her that all was good – she should just hang on and focus, because the pain was all in her mind. But I'm not entirely sure she believed that.

Suddenly, everything happened in a rush. The baby popped out, and I was astonished into total silence as I saw a small child with my own face looking back at me. The nurse asked if I'd like to cut her cord, but I was unable even to move, never mind cut, so she went ahead and completed it herself.

Simona and I were happy and relieved in a way that was beyond anything I could have imagined, and that moment changed everything for us. Having a baby daughter in the house, a mini-me in the bed, was awesome. I don't think I had realised that it would be the most fulfilling and exciting thing in my life.

When you have a kid, you change. You have to become more responsible, more careful, and even become a different couple. It was a turning point for us, but we knew we wanted two more children to complete a family of three. Yes, it's that Romanian folk-story number again!

Two boys followed their sister, with Stefan born in March 2012 and Serafim completing our squad in July 2016. I was present for both their births as well. They were a lot easier for both of us, as we knew the process and what to expect. But the one thing that remained just as intense was the incredible beauty of seeing the beginning of a new life as each child emerged into the world.

It is also fascinating to see how their individual personalities have evolved. I'm grateful we can give them the opportunities that neither of us were able to enjoy when we were children.

My dad only wanted me to do what he wanted me to do, which is why providing our children with the support and freedom to choose is the best gift we can give them. I still believe that the greatest teacher is life itself. When you make mistakes, you have to find out what went wrong and how to correct your own path. But I'll try to give them the best possible education, and I'm very proud of how they are all doing.

Sofia-Maria enjoys art and tennis and would like to be an architect. Stefan is more inclined towards IT; his room is like a miniature NASA with all the screens and speakers. Serafim is still very small but always curious. It will be intriguing to see where life takes each of them.

As our family grew, so did our business, mainly because our clients were happy with the quality of work we provided. This felt good, as I passionately believe it is important to be efficient, focus on excellence, and deliver projects on time and in budget.

Being based in London was a big advantage because the local companies we met from 2009 onwards were all major players in the industry. We built up our reputation with them through trust, delivery and value for money, which meant we also started getting new contracts through word of mouth – always the best way.

2013 was probably the game-changing year for us. The then mayor of London, Boris Johnson, decided that

TFL would reorganise all the different areas of the city and split them into three distinct infrastructure zones: Central, South-East and North-West. Each one would then award nine-year contracts to the major construction companies, who could subcontract the work to smaller partners.

That took us into a different place as a company. Instead of the relatively small-scale projects we'd been working on, we were now being trusted with delivering key parts of the major new development plans, including roads, traffic lights, bus routes and bridges. We also built the CS5, a cycle superhighway which goes from Victoria Station to the Oval via Vauxhall Bridge.

These new contracts accelerated our growth, because we had to update our systems and procedures. We also needed to deal with new aspects of the work that we'd never previously needed to know about. In human terms, these were our business's adolescent years, when we grew from a small local company to a fully-fledged and substantial business.

As we developed in size, we also needed to upgrade our premises and equipment. We had stretched well beyond the point where we could run the company from home with just the one trowel. We initially took a unit in nearby Kingsbury, close to Wembley Stadium, which came with some outdoor storage space. But in 2012 we moved a few miles away to Colindale.

We were based in a small yard behind a Mercedes dealership. Unfortunately, there was no admin space, so we put some containers together, refurbished them ourselves, and turned them into a very effective set of offices that served us well for almost seven years.

We were working in central London, and it was an exceptionally busy period. The traffic lights at junctions have a limited life-span, so the poles, cables, lights and controllers for signals all have to be upgraded every few years.

Our role was to carry out the civil element of the work, and prepare the sites for the engineers to come in and complete their jobs. We fulfilled projects in Kensington and Chelsea, Westminster, Holborn, Hyde Park Corner, Edgware and numerous other locations.

During that time, we recruited and built up a very experienced core team. There are so many dangers underground, so it is essential to employ people who know how to carry out all the key checks and map-reading before the digging even begins.

You might only see a curious patchwork of tarmac and concrete when you look at roads and pavements, but underneath that innocent-looking surface lies a chaotic ecosystem of pipes and cables, many going back a couple of centuries or longer. A spade or drill inserted in the wrong place can inconvenience a lot of people, while making a big dent in our profits.

The growth we experienced meant that Mears and other contractors now approached us with ever larger contracts and projects. This enabled us to continually expand through the 2010s. Eventually, we decided to move premises once again, to the much bigger site we are now based at in Borehamwood.

11

The Business of Business

In entrepreneurship and business, we all like to celebrate and proclaim our successes. But, as in other parts of life, there are plenty of times when things don't quite go to plan. I've certainly had my fair share of setbacks.

The failures came at different times, and for a variety of reasons. But the common themes seemed to be that I didn't have enough time to properly devote myself to a certain project, was spreading myself too thin, didn't have the right business partner, or was trying to expand into areas I just didn't know enough about.

When you build a business having grown up in poverty, I think you are always worried that it might all go wrong. That certainly applied to me. I'd had a lot of fear in childhood, and wanted to keep adding new dimensions to my business portfolio so that I'd have options if things turned bad.

One of our first businesses was doing very well – or at least it was until I took a break – but I think I am driven to constantly prove myself. In my mind, I hear my subconscious saying 'more, more, more' and 'build, build build'. I suspect a therapist would link this directly back to my father constantly telling me I'd never make it on my own.

Everything I tried seemed to be logical at the time. The projects that didn't come off have certainly been varied and – as all the business books say – we all learn from failure. So I've never been too depressed or upset when decisions didn't go as hoped.

Wild mushroom importation was an early example. One of my Romanian cousins suggested we start up a business together to import them from Eastern Europe to the UK. At that time, mushrooms were coming here via Italy and Germany, so we thought we would arrange for them to come directly into London and cut out the middle-men.

Unfortunately, it proved impossible to break into the business, as the existing chains and agreements were so strong, and we weren't able to source a high enough volume to make it financially viable. But it was an interesting experience, and we enjoyed cooking with some very tasty mushrooms. You fail, you learn, you drive forward.

I didn't have the option of studying business when I was at school, as all entrepreneurship was forbidden by Ceausescu. But from a young age I was interested in the thought of being able to create wealth. I wanted to reach a position where I could help other people, and develop a better environment.

Not surprisingly, my dad was completely against all forms of private enterprise. Having grown up in the Communist Party, he'd been brainwashed to believe that individual money was irrelevant. After the revolution occurred in 1989, a few things did begin to change in Romania, and I could see – even in my teens – that opportunities were starting to open. I remember one time suggesting to him that we should open a bar together in the village. I thought we could make a little money and use the profit to help out at home. But he gave me a withering look, as though I was crazy, and said he didn't want anything to do with such a foolish idea.

By 1993 and 1994, it was obvious that neighbours of ours were travelling to countries such as Turkey, Poland and Hungary so they could bring back previously unattainable goods, including much sought-after pairs of denim jeans.

They were clearly making money, as well as providing more options for local people. Although it was not something I could learn about at home or school, I could see there would be new opportunities for business in the future.

But I was young – just a child – and no-one really took me seriously. When my footballing idol, the legendary Gheorghe Hagi, and the rest of the Romanian team bleached their hair blond during the 1998 World Cup finals in France, I was so excited by the fact they were doing something controversial and different. But dad had been brought up never wanting to take a risk.

He thought their behaviour was ridiculous, as did football commentators around the world, as they struggled to identify 11 men with identical hairstyles.

His attitude was that you go to work, get your salary and that was it.

Be safe and secure, and don't throw any stones into a pond that could create ripples. That was the mentality of almost everyone from his generation in Romania and I gradually realised that I would have to fight against that restrictive and pessimistic outlook if I was going to live life in my own way.

Despite that lack of encouragement, or perhaps because of it, I set up a few small ventures on my own including selling Christmas trees. That was my first business. I found and cut the trees, and then delivered them to people in the village. I can still recall the feeling of power and control that gave me. For the first time in my life, I was earning my own money.

However, it wasn't until I moved to Portugal that my entrepreneurial instincts really came alive. I always thought I could see other and better ways of doing the work, managing the teams, and planning projects in a way that would make them more efficient and profitable.

Perhaps this was where my childhood came in useful, because I had sat and listened – even though I didn't often contribute – when my dad or grandad were talking. The nature of our society meant that, although children rarely offered opinions, we were always watching and listening. From an early age, we would be assessing potential risks to our family, and taking care not to say the wrong thing at the wrong time to the wrong person.

In a work environment, this flipped and became a positive attribute. I was able to soon see how important this ability is when it comes to management. Some managers don't listen to their teams; they just give orders and tell people to get on with their tasks, while taking no interest in new ideas or suggestions. They definitely don't want to hear about any problems.

But I came to realise that I'm different. I'll go in and I'll listen, and if someone has a valid point then I'll try and understand what they are going through and what their concerns are. Then, if necessary, I'll make changes. Useful, thoughtful feedback can make a huge difference, whether it benefits the client or ourselves or both.

If you don't listen to the people who are working with and for you, then you can't change and grow as a company or a boss. We all face real problems and unexpected challenges on every project, so it is essential that I know what the problematic issues are.

That is especially relevant in a period when we are all learning to deal with enormous external issues such as Covid, Russia's invasion of Ukraine, rising energy prices and the cost of living crisis. All these factors have combined to cause many problems with contracts, income, costs and supply.

On a more local level, time might be being wasted on a job because the team haven't got the correct information or equipment, or their tools are not fit for purpose. I expect everyone to tell me about anything that isn't working properly. Then I can go in with them to see for myself, and, if necessary, make the changes.

We know that football, tennis, golf and rugby are all played with balls, but each game requires a ball of different size and shape. It is the same for engineering. A client may say that he needs us to saw through something. But there are many different types of saw for all the varied materials and situations that we come across.

This is why it is so important that my employees know they should come to me as soon as there is a potential problem. The ability to refer problems upwards is something that was often lacking on the sites in Portugal. It was frustrating and infuriating to waste so much time. Ultimately, having a channel for feedback is simple common sense.

The same goes for the way we treat and speak with our staff. I'll never forget that, when I first came to England, I came across a man who had his own business, and who was relentlessly ruthless and rude towards his staff and clients. Before I left, I confronted him, and asked why he felt he had to be like that towards his team?

His answer, unsurprisingly, is not suitable for a book. But I thought his attitude was so stupid, as there is never any need to be like that. Having seen the impact his behaviour was having, and the way it demoralised everyone around him, I vowed I would always try to treat clients and staff in a respectful, polite and friendly manner. I knew that I could do better than him.

That said, I fully recognise that all workforces are a diverse group of individuals who are often motivated by very different things. For some people, the only consideration is how much money they will earn. For others it is about lifestyle. And, fortunately for us in my businesses, many also really care about the work they do, and the company that employ them.

A big part of my job, therefore, is to ensure we all work together as a team who feel safe, secure, respected and looked after. I have learned that the money-seekers will always move on, while others will stay, often for many years, as they care about the business and the work that we are doing with our clients.

That's why I have provided extra staff facilities in our Borehamwood headquarters. We have a well-equipped gym and a massage room available for anyone who wants to use them.

Many of the roles are physically arduous, so it is important we create places for the teams to work out, stay fit, meet their colleagues, and relax.

Wellbeing – in both a physical and mental sense – is a crucial responsibility of an employer, especially in this very challenging period. So I asked myself what I would like from my boss. After a little thought, I came up with the answer.

I'd like to be respected, to be communicated with, to be paid on time, and to be trusted. What's more, I'd prefer not to have my outside life questioned or pried into, and to have the chance to get fit and relax if I need to.

As a business owner, I can choose my management style. I have always felt that giving people more freedom as individuals, rather than being forced to follow strict and often petty sets of rules, creates an environment that is better for the staff, company and clients. And, ultimately, our profits and growth.

In general, our staff can start work or leave for home when they need, so long as they get the work done to the standard that we and our clients expect. And complete it on time, of course.

Over the years, I've found that this sort of flexibility

means people tend to be loyal and happy and want to get the jobs done. It is very important for me to be surrounded by these types of people, especially as it usually leads to an upbeat environment with a good atmosphere.

During the past decade and a half, I have learned numerous lessons and am still discovering new ways of working all the time. I know that sometimes I let my heart rule my head, especially if I like someone, and that led to me almost losing the business – as I alluded to in an earlier chapter.

A few years back, things were going well, and the main business had a turnover of about £7.5 million, so I took on a new business partner. I wanted to look at other opportunities and projects that we could start developing as a group in the UK and Romania, and I was happy to leave him in day-to-day charge.

At first, all seemed to be progressing smoothly. But then I began to get hints from concerned members of staff that there were an increasing number of problems. After some urgent meetings, I discovered that – far from continuing with our steady growth – turnover had actually dropped by almost 50 per cent.

I tried to find out what had happened, but he was very defensive, which was a huge disappointment. Not least because I had given him a large number of shares for free, assuming that would be a great motivator. But things had clearly not worked out.

This was a considerable lesson for me. I resolved never to take such a big step away again. I also began re-examining my whole approach to recruitment. I recognised it was essential that I took immediate action, as the accounts were due to be submitted, and I couldn't have the business being seen to have dropped to £3.7m or £4m.

That would look terrible when we were tendering for new contracts. The potential client would want to know what had caused the massive dip, and whether or not they could then risk working with us. The shortfall could be devastating if it remained uncorrected.

At a substantial personal cost, I bought out my then business partner, and took back total control of the day-to-day management of the company. I met my accountant to explore the available options, as I was completely confident that – despite the problems – the core business remained sound.

I was also encouraged to hear that there was a opportunity to apply for a three-month extension that would take us beyond the usual December due date for submitting our accounts, which would allow us more time to tackle the problems.

I started ringing all my contacts. I was desperate to find £1.5m of new contracts and rebuild our turnover back to at least £5.5m by the time our accounts were completed. I called everyone I knew, but I was struggling as nothing new seemed to be coming up. Then, just when I was on the point of accepting defeat, I found a potential breakthrough.

The very last name on my list was someone I was reluctant to speak to, because we'd had a falling out over a previous contract dispute. However, like all businessmen who want to be successful, I have learned that sometimes you have to give up your pride and do what is right for the business, rather than harbour any personal grudges or bad memories.

A part of me hadn't wanted to call him, because of what had happened in the past. But I knew he was a director of a company that might have work projects coming up. It was my lucky day, because at the time I called he just happened to have a £1.7m contract in Silvertown that he was about to tender. It proved to be exactly the lifeline we needed.

Others were also tendering for the same contract, but I was told there was still time to submit. Simona, our team and I worked flat out to get our pitch ready and in on time. On this occasion, the turnover was more important than the margins, so I priced it very competitively. To my great joy, we won it and we still made a decent profit after it was completed.

I could have done without the stress and cost of that experience, but it was also exhilarating to be able to find a solution so quickly that kept the business alive, enabling us to then grow steadily again. By 2019, I kept hearing that the next big thing for our industry would be fibreoptics, as the government had announced that they wanted to deliver ever faster and more reliable internet access right across the UK.

They started looking to the private utility companies, and I saw this as a massive opportunity. I decided that – because it was potentially long-term and lucrative and would provide many more jobs – I'd only work with people I believed in. People I trusted to work hard and creatively for the business and our colleagues.

When we were awarded a £180m contract to take on a large part of that new work, it was very satisfying. But also complex, as life beneath London's streets is often unpredictable. Still, it was worth doing. I want my kids and family to live in a nice city, and I know that the actions I take today will have an impact on whether they have a better or a worse future. We keep that in mind with the projects we accept, and the approach we take to the delivery.

As well as recruitment and staff wellbeing, there are many other aspects of business that I have to keep a close eye on, including our margins, as costs are going up every year. One example is insurance, as that has to cover so many different areas of our work. When we started out, we paid £7000 a year in insurance, which seemed a lot at that time. But by 2021, for example that figure had risen to half a million pounds.

And that is before a spade has gone into the ground, or a brick been laid. It is a very big pay-out for us to make each month before we open the gates. The whole team shares a responsibility to ensure we keep it as low as possible.

Despite the constant challenges, I have to admit that I love the thrill of business. Few things in life make me happier than landing deals and winning contracts. Finalising an agreement always gives me a real kick. For me, it is the business equivalent of scoring a goal, landing a knockout punch, or crossing the line first.

After all the anxiety and stress and preparation, there is a surge of adrenalin released when someone says yes. Then we shake hands on a project that will provide work for our teams, and help the company to grow.

I've also developed my own way of approaching meetings and rarely, if ever, take in notes. I prefer to do the work in advance, then rely on instinct and negotiation.

You have to get a feel for what the mood is, and how the possibilities could pan out.

It is important to be realistic and flexible, as I was able to demonstrate when we hit the turnover problem. And also to understand that sometimes we can't take on and beat the Goliaths, but have to work with and around them.

It is special to work in central London at so many iconic locations, such as in front of Buckingham Palace, and know that in our own small way we are contributing to the ever-evolving history of this amazing city. Creating infrastructure and seeing the result of our work makes me really happy.

I do it for the money as well, obviously. Yes, it is a business first and foremost – but it's also about being proud of what we do, and knowing that one day we can all tell our kids and grandchildren that we helped build this city.

I take the same approach with the houses and apartments that we are now building in the UK and in Romania, as we expand the property development side of our other businesses. I want them to all be perfect – from the design and foundations to the finish and decoration. When a potential buyer comes to see them for the first time, their first reaction should always be 'Wow'.

This philosophy is a part of who I am. With the building works, unlike some of my more personal decisions, I like things to be done properly and not rushed. I've thought back about this, and feel it may well come from my grandad, as he was always so meticulous – as with the fences that he straightened and painted every spring in Bukovina.

My feeling for business is very simple. Every deal has a break-even line. In the early years I came across so many people who were trying to pitch too low in order to get the contract, but always with the intention of adding in extra costs at a later date – when the client could no longer back out.

It is dishonest, and often means using fear as a tactic. That is something I would never do. I believe that a key part of our reputation and success has come because we are straightforward and honest. People like that.

I know what it's like to go into a meeting and feel someone trying to put pressure on you by the way they talk. As soon as I realise they are taking that approach, I know where they are coming from, what they want to achieve, and how I can counter it.

It's a natural intelligence and instinct, not something I believe you can learn at school or university. In business, you learn to get a feeling for these sorts of situations, and how to turn them to your advantage.

At the beginning, my biggest fear was being in business on my own. I lacked confidence, especially with the language. But the first few times I tried to find business partners, it didn't quite work out. So I made the decision to go it alone. When you are on your own, you can have the final say and make the deals you believe in.

I didn't know about that advice in my early years. I once had a partner who had good knowledge of the social-housing sector. As I had some money to invest, and was interested in that area, he convinced me to join him in a new partnership.

That was when I discovered how dangerous it is to

go into something you know little about. I had no clue about this one. At least with the mushrooms, there was a relatively low risk.

But this project initially cost me £300,000. I didn't understand about the timescale and the delivery lines, nor the requirements for items such as kitchen and bathroom furniture and equipment.

I reluctantly had to get involved myself, when the business hit major problems after I had provided the investment. But because I didn't know exactly what was going wrong, it was very confusing. I did a lot of research on Google, and contacted other contractors to ask questions.

I tried to learn very fast about key elements such as analysis, lead times, costings and how long it would take to fit things into place. The upshot was that, when we met to try and solve the problems, I was able to produce all my evidence and plans. This surprised him, and was very effective.

Because this particular project was collapsing into chaos, my priority was to identify and solve the core issues as quickly as possible. Preferably without losing any more money. I brought in people who could help me with their areas of expertise, as well as others who were already on site. I canvassed opinions and ideas.

I've always found that when people see your own commitment – and that you are rolling up your sleeves to do the best you can – they will come and help you. Some decisions were easy, such as the electrician who was taking unscheduled breaks to smoke dope on one of the balconies. He had been on our induction and knew what was expected, but made that decision himself, so I sacked him and that was one problem resolved immediately.

Fortunately, after a lot of hard work and a fair amount of stress, we ended up turning everything around at the development. We salvaged the contract, and it even made a nice profit when I eventually sold the business. That was about eight years ago. But, as we still weren't getting on well, it made sense to sell up and part company.

I love problem-solving. Practical and operational problems always fascinate. I can now see that I was heading in this direction even as a small child, as was illustrated when my grandma needed a new light and I worked out how to do it myself.

People often refer to 'lightbulb' moments when they get a new idea that solves a conundrum they've been struggling with. For me, the term could be taken literally, because that was where it all started. More recently, we've had to deal with a lot of the unexpected puzzles I've already mentioned. We have no option but to find solutions ourselves.

Harold Macmillan was the British prime minister between 1957 and 1963. When asked what was the most difficult aspect of his job, he replied '*events, dear boy, events*'. That response perfectly sums up the challenges of business.

Leaders need to be patient, flexible, calm, decisive, creative and determined. Especially as the vast majority of the problems they face will have been created by something or someone else, as the 2020s have unfortunately demonstrated so regularly.

Another key aspect of leadership is the desire to constantly ask why? Or – even better – why, how, when?

I can never accept anything on face value, but I know this can sometimes annoy people. I remember that when I was taking out my first mortgage, I was asking the broker many questions, even about how much commission he was making from my deal, and he became quite irritated with me.

But it is only by asking lots of questions that you can uncover the details required to inform your judgment. That curiosity also leads into the need to be efficient, and adapt to changing situations. For example, when Boris Johnson – who was then mayor of London – announced that the Low Emission Zone (LEZ) would be extended from January 2012, we realised that the new daily charges and potential fines would cost us a lot of money. We had a growing fleet, and many of the vans were at least a decade old.

It was a very worrying time. I didn't have the capital to suddenly just go out and buy lots of brand-new vehicles. That would have cost hundreds of thousands of pounds. I knew that I had to think laterally if I was to find a solution that would enable us to continue working in London. So I spent my evenings surfing online, in the hope that I'd spot something that would trigger a solution.

Fortunately, something did indeed come up – and from a source that I would never otherwise have dreamed could be an option. I saw an advert for an auction of milk lorries. Built in 2005 and 2006, these vehicles essentially consisted of just a chassis and a cab, with a flat base where the churns were held in place by chains. Because they were such specialist items, they were selling for only about £1200 each.

As I looked at the photos, I realised I could add panels on to the side and back, and turn them into dropside vans. So I bought 27 of them from all around the UK – including sites as far apart as Scotland and Exeter. I found a factory in Wales who added the panels at a cost of around £700 each, and when we painted them, they were perfect. One month later, the new restrictions came in, and suddenly we had a fleet of vehicles ready to go.

Our clients and competitors were stunned as they assumed we must have spent at least £15,000 for each vehicle. But instead of an outlay of £400,000, it had only cost us around £50,000 in total, with each lorry coming in at about £1750 each. I then financed them to improve the cash flow for the business, so we could reinvest that back into new staff and plant.

The finance company valued the new fleet at £420,000 and gave me 70 per cent, which we used to grow the business further and faster. I remember that very clearly as it was one of the best and most important deals I've done. It came out of my own research and initiative, and from asking 'Why can't we find a cheaper way?'

It would obviously be impossible for me to be involved in every single day-to-day decision, but I am always across the business and like to know everything that is going on. My mental checklist includes keeping an eye on our contracts, spotting problems early, cutting the bullshit, making sure all the different departments and partners talk to each other, and delivering quality projects on budget and in time for our clients.

Risk management is another very important element of business. In the past, I would sometimes run into a big problem when clients suddenly refused to pay, tried to delay the terms, or even wanted refunds at the end of the contract.

As a direct result, one of the major developments we've made as a company is that we are always trying to mitigate the risk of not being paid. Defaulting clients can have a devastating impact, and even more so in times of wider economic uncertainty.

Before we sign them, all our contracts undergo multiple legal discussions and checks to head off potential issues. But the biggest risk factor these days is that big corporations can make you work for two years with an open contract.

You agree some heads of terms, then as you go along you put in an interim valuation to get paid. The problem is that they reserve the right, two months or two years down the line, to revoke one item. This can cause a massive disturbance, and a potentially significant loss.

What I do now, in order to manage the risk, is to make sure we are paid well in advance. That way, if we experience this type of situation again in the future, we'll be covered. Or, at worst, we'll only stand to possibly lose five or ten per cent of the contract's value instead of 80 per cent.

I have met far too many people who used to run their own firms, but went under because they didn't get paid. For some reason, this is especially prevalent in the UK. It is one of the biggest problems that we have to be aware of and plan for.

Newcomers can sometimes enter the business world with lots of enthusiasm but little or no experience. They then encounter some of the big firms who have no mercy or scruples. As in the oceans, the big fish kill and devour the little ones.

I always try to stand up against these corporate great white sharks. They don't like it and accuse me of bullying them, or holding a gun to their head. But I'm not. I'm just protecting the company and my employees' jobs.

They have rents and mortgages and families, and they depend on my decisions. I have built our businesses myself from nothing. I didn't inherit money, and the companies are a result of our hard work. I am always very straight and fair, so if I do the job as agreed, then I expect to get paid.

That is probably the ultimate example of why risk management is so important. The main responsibility all bosses have is to avoid their company becoming bankrupt. In my experience, some 90 per cent of the people who fail in business don't understand these pitfalls and didn't plan for them, but I would say that avoiding non-payers is a very high percentage of my job.

It isn't sexy, it sounds dull, but it is so important. We do the same in life every day when we check to see if the road is clear or that our windows are shut or that the children stay away from sharp knives. Safety protocols are therefore a natural part of business as well.

The approach we take sometimes changes from client to client. Fortunately, I've never had to go to court. But we have occasionally had to chase up slow payers by issuing legal threats. The construction industry has historically operated with a lot of verbal agreements, which can mean it is very hard to resolve disputes because of a lack of written evidence. In this situation, a judge will refer to adjudication and arbitration, but that is something we have changed because we aim to have everything agreed in writing.

In 2020, I had many distractions. Apart from all the changes we had to make because of Covid, I was also spending time in Romania during my father's final illness. It came as a very unpleasant shock at the end of the year to discover that one client still owed us £4.7m. It took a massive battle and a lot of time to get it paid up in full.

If we ever reach that point in the future, we will give the client a clear choice. Either we get paid – as per the contract – or we stop the work. If we had gone to court, it would have cost me half a million in legal fees, so it came as a big relief when it was all sorted. But I never want to feel so exposed again.

That caution extends to our work in Romania. When I was agreeing the contracts for my new construction projects in Bucharest, I took into account the issues and lessons learned from the dreadful fire at Grenfell Tower in London. On June 14, 2017, a fire started by a faulty refrigerator spread into the cladding and the insulation of the whole block. Because of poor safety standards, 72 people were tragically killed.

In Bucharest, I wanted extra checks on the company who were providing the cladding. I wanted to double-check their insurance and accounts, as well as their certification. I had nightmares about building the block, and then losing everything because the cladding company had gone bust and vanished. And I hoped to make the buildings as safe as possible for the owners of the new apartments.

When I was a child, we lived a world of such relentless secrecy and conspiracy that risk assessment was a subconscious and constant part of our childhood. Fear of the Securitate, and what we could accidentally say or reveal, were always in our minds. So maybe that sort of caution has become a natural part of me.

It had a massive impact, as I had to look at everything differently from most of the people I know who grew up in Britain. I realise that I can take on too much, in Romania as well as the UK, but if I hit a problem I deal with it and find a solution. I don't panic, and that is a part of my personality I'm very grateful for.

As well as the impact my childhood had on my approach to business, living in the UK has also taught me so much, and enabled me look at things differently. I try to always keep up with the financial press and media. The Financial Times is one of the best places for relevant news.

Nowadays information can come from many different sources, good and bad, so it is important to be always trying to look two steps ahead. I'm constantly seeking out opportunities to grow the company.

It might seem strange that, when our businesses are doing well, and have a very healthy bank balance and valuation, we should be working even harder to plan for the future. But that is what is needed for survival and growth.

You always have to be thinking ahead and preparing where possible for Harold Macmillan's 'events'. Even though we don't know for certain what they will be, we know they will come head on at us at some stage. No matter what your expertise or business is, there will always be unforeseen circumstances that have to be dealt with.

A phrase I was made familiar with when I moved to London was '*by failing to prepare, you are preparing to fail.*' It was first attributed to the American scientist, inventor and stateman Benjamin Franklin, but was also famously used by the former England and Essex cricket captain Graham Gooch when he was rebuilding the national side. It is especially relevant to business as well.

Brexit is a good example. At one of our main businesses we employ a staff of around 180 at any one time. Forty of these are permanent. The others are contracted for specific jobs and roles. By the time the cut off from Europe arrived, 90 per cent of our staff were British or had settled status. We had a handful of guys who didn't sort it out in time, but most did, and we helped them to plan ahead.

Simona's involvement is absolutely key to the company's healthy situation as well. So my final tip for business success is to have a wonderful partner you can trust. When we had our children, she took a step back while they were very young. But she is far more involved on a daily basis again, and during the past five years has played a crucial role.

Her involvement includes: keeping across spending and payments, overseeing invoices to check against possible overcharging, chasing staff on fines and parking, checking in on transport and plant, double-checking wages and timesheets, and much more. She does a great job, and without her we wouldn't be in as strong a position. I'd say that, in five years, Simona has saved the company at least half a million pounds.

She also monitors the fuel expenditure, as we spend £44,000 a week to keep everything running. It is a cost that has substantially increased in recent times, and may have gone up a lot more by the time you read this.

Fortunately, we invested in a major storage facility that holds 18,000 litres, so we were able to get through the crazy and unnecessary crisis period of closed garages and fuel shortages during September and October 2021. The extra storage has also left us in reasonable shape for the further fuel-supply challenges that came along in 2022 and 2023, even though soaring prices have hit everyone hard.

In the autumn of 2021, the petrol crisis was most definitely an 'event', albeit one that should never have happened. The panic was created by a mix of Covid and the tanker-driver shortage caused by Brexit, but it was hardly helped by the words of the then Secretary of State for Transport, Grant Shapps, when he appeared on national TV and radio.

Shapps came on to assure the nation that there were no shortages. No sooner had he spoken than the British public jumped into their cars, formed long queues at petrol stations, and ensured that large parts of the country ground to a halt!

Other than the current crisis of rising utility prices and interest rates, the next big challenge will be the switch to electric vehicles. We are already looking at options for our vans and lorries, and asking how we can create the infrastructure to charge them up overnight in the yards.

On one recent exercise we carried out, we worked out that with electric vehicles and no congestion charge, we'd save many thousands of pounds each month. But against that is the prospect of new charges being introduced for each mile driven.

Then there are the problems with battery life, and the need to actually get to and from the sites. Although we know people are working on that, electric vans still lack the range of petrol or diesel vehicles. For us, the biggest cost of all will be the need to replace the majority of the fleet. The vehicles cannot be converted and the price-tag is likely to run into several millions of pounds.

One major issue we face is with powering our grab lorry. We will almost certainly have to install our own charging station in central London, since the infrastructure for vehicles that size has not yet been developed yet. Indeed, it is unlikely to come onstream for some considerable time, because the existing underground cables can't handle the power that will be required.

All of these changes will have a big impact on millions of businesses. We all have to cope with adapting to new green legislation, increased labour charges, and shortages and problems with the materials and supply chains.

That said, business is still a wonderful and exciting world to operate in. As well as the key areas I've highlighted in this chapter, I'd advise any young person who is thinking of starting their own company to believe in yourself. You can succeed if do your research, work hard, treat everyone with respect, and never give up.

12

Other Ventures

Earlier I mentioned that I'd once, briefly, ventured into the world of wild mushroom importation. Along the way there have been a few other similar businesses that didn't quite work out, and for similar reasons.

A friend of mine has a couple of successful wooden-floor showrooms in the UK and Romania. He knew of someone back home who was making good quality sofas, so we thought that maybe people who were buying floors might want furniture at the same time. They didn't.

The importation of Romanian timber was another idea that proved to be too complicated and time-consuming, despite the links I had with all the villages in Bukovina and the local forests. So I dropped that as well.

Cars, however, are a different matter. They are my hobby – a subject that I love and know a lot about. In the UK, it is very easy for people to own and upgrade cars on a regular basis because of all the finance options that are available. The sales market is dominated by the Auto Trader group.

Originally founded in 1975 by John Madejski, Auto Trader soon became a very well-known and popular magazine. It was published in different regions around the UK, before being launched as a highly successful online version as well.

I thought that, despite Auto Trader's market dominance, there might be room for an additional online portal for people looking to buy and sell cars and other vehicles. So I launched AutoVolo in 2015. Someone else runs it for me, and we are making steady progress, but it has been a tougher challenge than I expected. It is a very large and competitive industry, and requires a lot of money to be spent on advertising.

With this particular project, I learned that passion is not always enough. As with the social housing experience, you should never go into a business where you have not experienced it yourself first-hand, and don't know how it works.

By contrast, with civil engineering I have done literally every job myself at some stage. I was still out working on sites until very recently, so I know the business from every angle. But with cars, I know it mainly as a consumer and enthusiast.

I also learned that the British car market is very conservative. If people have grown up with Auto Trader and always used it, they will be loyal to the brand. It can take a long time for a new player to become an established alternative, especially without a major financial backer.

The Transylvanian city of Cluj-Napoca, also just known as Cluj, is the fourth largest city in Romania. In 2017, we started a car rental company – Volo Rentacar – that is doing very well. We began with eight vehicles and rapidly grew to more than 40, although the arrival of Covid 19 meant we had to rapidly change our business model.

As so many people were locked down, we started working with shops and restaurants which needed a fleet for their home deliveries. We hired out 14 cars during that period, and that helped cover some of our own costs.

It is very important to have the right team in place when you are not able to be there regularly yourself. Fortunately, we have an excellent set of employees, led by a very enthusiastic, young and talented guy called George. We'd now like to expand into Bucharest, and other areas of Romania.

I know the area very well, because when I was 14 my sister Ana was admitted to a hospital in Cluj for an operation. As my parents were both unable to leave home because of work and family commitments, I was given the task of taking food and clothes to her. It was a massive undertaking for me, and I was scared of traveling as it was so far from home, but I fell in love with the city and it was unlike anywhere I'd ever experienced before.

When Simona and I married, we decided that it would be a good time to invest in Romania. The economy was beginning to show signs of growth, as the world finally emerged from the global financial crisis and the country became a part of the enlarged European Union.

We also wanted to create something for ourselves that was away from our families and the area where we had both grown up and spent our childhoods.

Following the recession in 2009, a lot of apartments became available at a low cost. So we took out some mortgages and purchased 12 of them. After renovating them, we let them for a few years, and eventually managed to sell them at double the cost.

We were then able to reinvest the profit in another new project: the erection of a small 18 room hotel close to Cluj airport. Called Volo House, it is aimed at the short-stay business market, and we hope to start expanding into other parts of the country as well.

As I've suggested before, success in business requires you to have good knowledge, plan well, take control, and know what outcome you want. In the businesses that haven't worked out, I was often depending too much on other people and their supposed specialist knowledge. That wasn't always enough. But I was young, and I learned from all the failures and mishaps, which is the most important thing.

Having gained so much experience in construction, we are now building apartments in Romania and the UK. I have decided that my main business focus for the next stage will be on civil engineering, and building real estate and hotels.

They share many similar characteristics, and are both worlds that I am very comfortable in, not least because they often involve creating something completely new. That always gives me a thrill – when I see a project grow from an initial idea on a piece of paper to something that many people can use every day.

I'm always inspired by people who take risks to help the progress of humanity. It is something I often see in the worlds of cars and racing. Their development teams are always seeking ways of making vehicles safer, more efficient and more environmentally friendly.

It is amusing to think back to when cars first arrived in England. In 1865, the government passed the Locomotive Act – also known as the red-flag act. It stipulated that self-propelled vehicles should be accompanied by a crew of three, that a man with a red flag was to walk at least 55m ahead of each vehicle, and that it was required to stop at the signal of the flagbearer.

Now we are at the exciting next stage of development where electric and self-drive cars will be the future. I believe that, by 2030, we will see amazing and efficient vehicles that will have less impact on the environment.

One of my favourite stories is that of Enzo Ferrari, who followed his dream to build the fastest cars ever. He took the best engineer in Italy from Fiat, even though everyone wanted him, and started his company from scratch. Ferrari went on to build the cars that took on the world.

He followed his dream, and is a great example to entrepreneurs. We all know that the road can be hard, and is littered with many obstacles. But you have to keep going forward, to overcome the challenges and the negativity, if you are to reach your goals.

However, another lesson that I've learned is not to overstretch yourself and take on too many different things. It is important to keep a good work-life balance, and not miss out on your children growing up.

There can be many opportunities in business, but there is only one chance to see your child walk for the first time. That said, I don't want to reach the end of my life and regret not having tried something. Yes, I realise that is the legacy of my dad speaking to me, even today. But I try things, and if they don't work out then I move on. The clichés are all true, and the process of trying can be a lot of fun, even when it doesn't go entirely as planned.

That was almost the case with the first home Simona and I bought together, a couple of years after we got married. It was a house that had been on the market for more than half a year on a former council estate in Broadfield in North London. It had a terrace and nice neighbours, but needed a lot of work to bring it up to date.

I employed a Romanian labourer to help me, as there was so much to do. On one of the first days he was on site, I told him I was going to the shops to pick up some food for our lunch. Having handed him a sledgehammer, I gave him specific instructions to knock down the single wall that made the hall too narrow and dark.

I still don't really know how the communications went so badly wrong, but when I returned I found that he'd demolished almost all the downstairs walls, and was about to start on the chimney as well! If I hadn't come back when I did, there was a very real danger that the house would have caved in and collapsed.

I was completely shocked, as I couldn't understand how anyone could be that stupid. Then I also had to face Simona, who – not surprisingly – was extremely unhappy to come home and discover a downstairs that was now almost entirely open-plan. The labourer was paid off quickly, and I had to start shoring up the building as fast as I could, rebuilding the walls with the help of some friends.

Having originally paid £250,000, we spent another £40,000 on developing the house and drive. It looked superb, and we had some happy times there. We were even happier when we sold it for a profit of £140,000.

After that, we bought and did up a few properties that we let out for a period before selling them. We then reinvested the profit to grow the business, and wound up with an increasing interest in property.

We've lived in our current home in Wembley for several years. Because it is close to a Romanian Orthodox Church, it is somewhere I'd wanted to live for a long time. We bought it from the children of a Hungarian tailor who had lived there for four decades.

But when some of my neighbours discovered we were Romanian, they made some wrong assumptions, and objected to all the planning applications I submitted to the council for renovations. The building was tired, and we wanted to make some changes that would suit our family.

I became so fed up with the situation that I eventually told a local estate agent I had decided to give up and rent the property for 12 months to a travelling family with horses, who were looking for local accommodation with a garden. I asked him to draw up an appropriate contract.

This was a cunning ploy. I also knew that the same estate agent was friends with my neighbours. As I had hoped and expected, they soon got to hear about the new plans and withdrew their planning objections. Now we are all very good friends.

13

Politics

This is an area I've become ever more interested in, dipping a toe into the very different waters of Romanian and British politics. I'd like to gain experience of campaigning to learn how to create new and useful policies, and to do something where I am in a position to help others. Much as we are planning to do with the Corporate Social Responsibility programmes for our businesses.

There are very few Romanian politicians I admire, but when I first came to England, I partly learned English by listening to some of the speeches by the former British prime minister Margaret Thatcher. I discovered them on YouTube, along with speeches by other politicians.

They are often very interesting. The art of rhetoric is a valuable one. When a speech is written by an expert who knows how to use the rhythm of language, it is so much more effective at transmitting ideas. I found these videos incredibly useful, even if this might seem a surprising way of picking up a new language.

Despite that, for most of my first 35 years I had very little interest in politics, especially in the UK. I didn't know anyone who was involved, had no real understanding of the different parties and their policies, and was too busy with my own work to give it much attention. But then, in 2019, that began to change. I felt a deepening need to find out more.

In Romania, the very mention of the word politics usually prompted a reaction of contempt and distrust when I was growing up – or perhaps even fear. The long years of communism and authoritarian rule, with their endemic corruption and the terror created by the Securitate, had left us with a deep-seated hostility towards politicians. The main approach of most people I knew at home was that politics should never be mentioned.

My impression is that, even though Ceausescu has gone, many or most of his henchmen have simply rebranded themselves as democrats. They adopted new party names that would appeal to the West and then carried on much as before.

Corruption is still a Romanian disease that looks very hard to cure. Great chunks of our industry and land were sold to other nations, a small number of officials and government ministers have become very wealthy, and the lives of the majority – especially in regions like Bukovina – are often left behind.

But gradually, as our businesses grew and I encountered an increasing number of planning and construction issues through my negotiations with councils, I realised that politics and policy did matter. I started to feel that I should find out more and began to educate myself.

I knew that I needed to start at the beginning – as I did with all our projects – and find out how politics in the UK actually worked at the most local level. It proved to be a lot more complicated than I had realised or expected.

For Romanian readers, I've given you a basic outline of how it works in in the same way that I gave a short guide to Romanian history for British readers.

Britain is a parliamentary democracy with a constitutional monarchy where everyone over the age of 18 is entitled to vote in general elections. But the system is often very illogical and hard to follow.

Instead of a written constitution, there are a series of traditions, conventions and rules that have evolved over the centuries since the arrival of William the Conqueror in 1066. I am sure there are scholars who will tell me that some laws and rules go back even further, but there is a limit to how much a newcomer can take in!

At first glance, it looks as though there are many similarities between the Romanian and British political systems. Both have a head of state, a separate prime minister and a parliamentary system that consists of two houses.

There are also, however, a great many differences. The Romanian president is elected by the people for a five-year term, whereas the British have a hereditary head of state. Queen Elizabeth II – who was on the throne for 70 years until her death on September 8, 2022 – was succeeded by her 74-year-old eldest son. King Charles

III can trace his family line of monarchs back for many centuries.

The Romanian parliament has a Chamber of Deputies with 330 members, and a Senate with 136 members, each elected for four-year terms using a system of closed party-list proportional representation. The prime minister of Romania is proposed by the president and voted upon by parliament. He or she will either be the leader of the majority party or, where the vote is split, someone who can command a majority.

In the UK, there are 650 members of parliament (MPs) in the House of Commons. Each represents an individual constituency in England, Scotland, Wales or Northern Ireland. They are elected in a first-past-the-post system, where the person with the most votes in each constituency wins the seat and enters parliament.

Since the end of World War II British politics has been dominated either by the right-of–centre Conservative Party or the left-leaning Labour Party. The prime minister is the leader of the winning party at the general election. (In other words, the party which has the most seats.)

The Liberal Democrats are the traditional third party, who sit somewhere between Labour and the Conservatives in their political values. But the only time in more than a century that they have been in power was during the 2010-2015 coalition.

In addition, you have the Scottish Nationalist Party – who now dominate in Scotland – several smaller nationalist parties in Wales and Northern Ireland, and a single Green MP.

The Houses of Parliament at Westminster are known around the world as the Mother of Parliaments and the home of democracy. Yet they still have an unelected House of Lords. This is the second largest legislative chamber in the world. Only the Chinese National People's Congress has more members.

In 2023, the House of Lords consists of 92 hereditary peers, all men, who have inherited their title and seat when a family member has died. There are also 26 Church of England bishops and archbishops, plus 668 life peers. The people in this last group are given special titles. They are a curious mix of former politicians, scientists, lawyers, entertainers and sportspeople. They usually represent one of the main parties but can also sit as independents.

Its role is as a revising chamber which scrutinises legislation proposed by the elected House of Commons. It can temporarily block legislation and suggest amendments, but it doesn't have the power to stop a government from doing what it wants. Once a piece of legislation has been finally voted through in each House, it becomes law when it has been signed by the King.

Britain has multiple levels of local democracy, including many different types of council. These range from the tiny parish councils, which look after local village issues in rural areas, to the large metropolitan councils that run the major cities and towns.

For many years, I have lived in the North London district of Wembley. This counts as part of the London borough of Brent – one of 32 London boroughs which each has its own elected council. For most of the world, Wembley is mainly associated with the famous football stadium. But there is also a vibrant multicultural community with a very large number of immigrants, especially from Asia.

Since it was formed in 1965, the council has had a Labour majority for 49 years, and a Conservative majority for just three years between 1968 and 1971. Labour have led the council since 2010. In the most recent elections in 2022, they won 49 of the 57 available seats. The Conservatives won five, and the LibDems the remaining three.

The ethnicity of the borough is very interesting, and the immense diversity would be completely alien to many who are used to living in Romania. In 2019, it was estimated that – of a population of almost 330,000 in the borough of Brent – only just over a third were white.

Of these, 18 per cent were listed as white British, with four per cent white Irish and 14.3 per cent white other, including many Romanians who have settled in the area. The Asian population was estimated to make up 34 per cent of the borough, with the Black Afro–Caribbean population supplying 15.4 per cent.

As I said, I have lived in the area for many years. But as the world evolved, and issues such as Brexit and climate change came to dominate the political agenda, I felt that I needed to become a participant rather than just a spectator.

I'm concerned about the future of my children, my business and my staff. And, of course, my homeland. But as so much of my work is related to local infrastructure, I thought that maybe I could start by becoming involved with my local politics in Wembley. However, when I started to take an interest, I found myself entering a completely new world.

First, I needed to decide which party I supported, and whose politics I thought were closest to mine. At local level in London, it was a straight choice between Labour and Conservative. No-one else has a chance of winning a seat, especially if they are an independent.

The easiest path would have been to join the Labour Party. It was during the premiership of Tony Blair that Romania was accepted into the European Union. It was as a result of Labour's support for Romania that I was able to travel to England in 2007, start my company, develop a business, and be in a position to write this book.

I am learning, however, that life is not always simple – especially where the subject of politics is concerned. While living in London, I also saw the Labour Party swing from the more centrist and business-friendly governments of Blair and Brown to the soft-left socialism of Ed Miliband, their leader in opposition from 2010 to 2015.

Next came their disastrous period under the left-winger Jeremy Corbyn. His election as leader – which happened in 2015 – came as a complete shock to the majority of Labour MPs and traditional members.

Corbyn's rise stunned everyone. It derived from a controversial and ill-thought-out new voting system, introduced by his predecessor Miliband. This allowed anyone to join the Labour Party for £3 and vote in the leadership election, even if they didn't support the policies of the party. In 2019, Corbyn led Labour to their worst defeat in a general election since 1935 and resigned.

The more I learned and understood, the more I realised that the Conservatives were a party I felt a lot more at home with. Even though I realised that their electoral prospects in Brent were bleak at best.

Still, I remain a huge admirer of Thatcher. During her 11 years as a Conservative prime minister, she was one of the most important global political figures. Then she was thrown out of office by her own MPs. This was a poor way of showing gratitude for three enormous election victories.

Even now, more than three decades after she left power, Thatcher is a very polarising figure in British politics. She inspires reverential adoration on the right and contemptuous hatred on the left. My own position is influenced by two key parts of her legacy, which I believe have played crucial roles in my life and career.

The first is the way that small businesses have been encouraged to develop, build and grow since the Thatcherite revolution of the early 1980s. The second is the way her administration, with policies of privatisation and deregulation, created an environment that enabled companies like mine to exist today.

Just as importantly – if not more so – she led the way throughout the 1980s in standing up to the failing communist regimes of Eastern Europe. Working closely with the American president Ronald Reagan, and forging a unique relationship with the Soviet leader Mikhail Gorbachev, Thatcher changed the world.

Glasnost in Russia represented the defining moment of a process in which terror and repression in that part of the world was swept away, at least for several decades.

One by one, authoritarian regimes fell in Poland, East Germany, Czechoslovakia, Hungary, Bulgaria and

Romania. Then the USSR disintegrated, allowing countries such as Lithuania, Latvia, Estonia and Ukraine to regain their freedom as sovereign nations.

The Conservative Party is still a champion of small business, so I joined them online in August 2019. I already knew some of the local members, and started finding out more about my local constituency.

I was very impressed with their passion and dedication to improving the lives of local people, despite being so massively outnumbered by the Labour Party in Brent. I enjoyed taking part in several local initiatives including litter collections in the nearby parks.

I was flattered and surprised when, after just a few months of membership, I was invited to stand as one of two Conservative candidates for Brent Council in the Barnhill ward. This was close to my home, where a by-election had been called following the resignation of two councillors. For several winter nights, I came home from work and put leaflets through doors, campaigned, met local people, and worked closely with my Conservative colleagues.

Unfortunately, it is a common feature of local elections in the UK that turnout can be very low. As the country had just had its third general election in five years – in addition to the Brexit referendum – we suspected that the electorate would be suffering from ballot box fatigue, and knew that every vote would count.

When voting day arrived – January 23, 2020 – we were quietly confident that we would have a good chance of success. We chased up as many of our known supporters as possible to encourage them to vote for me and my colleague Kanta Mistry.

It was a cold and miserable day in North London, and unfortunately only 22 per cent of those who were eligible actually left their homes to put a cross against the names of their preferred representative. Two Labour candidates were narrowly elected to represent the area.

Kanta and I were convinced that 100 votes for us had been wrongly placed in the Labour pile. We had to challenge the result in the High Court because, on the night of the election, the Brent Council chief executive Carolyn Downs ignored our protests and refused to allow a recount.

Despite what we believed was strong evidence that a missing bag of ballots could have made a difference to the outcome – and the fact that an unsealed sack of ballots with no markings to confirm which election they related to was later discovered – we were unfortunately unsuccessful in our appeal. The judgment went against us on February 19, 2021.

I was very unhappy with the circumstances, and the way the whole thing was handled, especially as I believe that free, fair and transparent elections are the backbone of our democracy. But I had no option but to accept the ruling of the High Court.

During the next 18 months, I did try to help the local association where possible. I was proud to be made the deputy chair of membership for Brent North Conservative Association. But I had less and less time available to devote to local politics.

My attention was absorbed by a combination of family illness, steering our business through Covid 19, and then just trying to keep the business afloat as – like so many companies – we were hit by a huge and sudden crisis in our supply chain.

I was also discovering the frustrating reality that it takes a lot longer to reach a decision and take action in politics than it does in business. Across our business, we have meetings that reach conclusions and authorise action, whereas in politics so much time seemed to be spent having meetings about meetings, discussing procedure, and making allowances for different personalities. These already slow processes were often further disrupted by personal disputes and grievances.

On the upside, I made some good friends. There are many people in the Conservative Party I admire hugely – such as Bob Blackman, the MP for Harrow East – because of their genuine passion for helping the people in our area, and doing all they can to make their lives better.

In 2022 I stood again, this time in the Edgware ward for Harrow Council. Unfortunately, I lost out again by just 79 votes, although I am extremely proud of our campaign to encourage members of the Romanian diaspora to register to vote and thus engage in the local democratic process. I hope that many more of them do so in the future as well.

In 2023 I was very proud to be nominated by the majority of local Conservative Party members to be their candidate in the Brent and Harrow constituency for the London Assembly elections that will take place in May 2024. I look forward to campiagning with all my colleagues across the constituency as we raise crucial local issues and hope to return a Conservative member in the seat for the first time in 20 years.

In 2020, I was also persuaded to stand for one of the seats in the Romanian Senate that are reserved for the seven million diaspora who are now living and working around the world. I was well aware of the difficulties that an independent candidate faced, when up against the organising might of the main parties. But I thought it was important that someone should at least be flagging up some of the issues that Romanians who have left the country can face.

All 136 seats were contested on December 6, including two to represent voters from the diaspora. It is estimated that approximately 30 per cent of the nation's population now live out of the country, including more than one million Romanians who have moved to the UK.

Here was another very valuable experience. My manifesto pledges were to assist Romanian people with better representation, support, education, pensions and job opportunities. I wanted to encourage them to return home to Romania. I hoped that they would be able to reintegrate, using their newly acquired skills, languages and wealth to help build a better long-term future for the country.

I didn't win, but I gained so much knowledge about the process – both good and bad – that would have been impossible to pick up in any other way. My approach to politics has been the same as the one I've previously explained about business. It is essential to know as much as possible about any new area if you want to make a success of it.

My ventures into the British and Romanian elections achieved exactly that – a deeper understanding. I have a much clearer idea of the processes involved. That means being able to plan the right strategies for media, marketing, and finances. And, of course, being wise to the danger of dirty tricks.

I have also discovered that politics could learn lessons from business. One of my central insights is very straightforward, and seems to me to be common sense, since you won't get far without appointing the right people to do the key jobs. It can be summarised in five words: don't keep reshuffling your team.

The problem with some political leaders is that they don't listen to professionals who have experience or expertise in certain fields. They seem to place party loyalty and ideological soundness above competence and ability.

Ministers in both countries also tend to change jobs so frequently that they are unable to make any useful long-term impact. No sooner have they managed to understand their department, and started thinking usefully about the problems they face, than they are moved elsewhere, and have to begin all over again.

Just one is example in the UK is the department responsible for education. There have been 10 different secretaries of state attending cabinet in the past 13 years. That must make it impossible for any of them to really understand their incredibly important brief, or achieve anything meaningful.

In business, that would be regarded as farcical and illogical – a self-defeating waste of time and resources., And yet, the very people whose laws we follow would seem to regard that absurd process as completely normal. And in the latter half of 2022 we had four chancellors of the exchequer in just four months, as the Boris Johnson and Liz Truss governments lurched from crisis to crisis.

How would any business expect to have stability if they changed the chief financial officer every few weeks? By contrast, Britain's previous five chancellors had collectively been in office for 23 years.

Leadership should not be about ego or money, but about making a difference. Leaders need to help themselves and others to do the right things by setting the direction, building visions, and so creating something new. Being in government should be dynamic, exciting and inspiring – and not just a means of helping friends and making money.

It may well be that my own future is in politics, but my current role is still primarily that of a businessman and I'm confident that side of my life is looking good. We have a lot of work on the books. For example we have already begun focussing on the next major series of works in London, which is the installation of new charging points for electric vehicles. This requires the biggest underground infrastructure revamp ever to be attempted in the city as the existing cables are not capable of carrying the kind of power needed to charge cars and vans for Londoners.

The fibreoptic roll out will still grow for a few more years, but charging points for electrical cars will be a massive part of the future for companies such as ours. It is also the main reason why we are staying based in London. Despite the massive costs we incur, we have the huge benefit of deep local knowledge. There is barely a borough we haven't worked in at some stage.

Even so, when you operate a fleet of 50 or 60 trucks, the many new charges – such as ULEZ – can become extremely expensive. So we are also looking at working in locations such as Berkshire and West Sussex, in order to diversify slightly.

We did try once doing some work in Ipswich, but it was very challenging to find qualified staff who were not already employed and secure in their existing jobs. To make things even harder, freelancers who were based in London didn't want to travel that far each day.

We moved here to our current home in Borehamwood because the business was steadily growing, and the site we rented in Colindale had been sold. We used a warehouse in Brent Cross for a short period, and then a friend told me about this empty and rundown building, with its own substantial yard.

It was in a dreadful state, having been vandalised, trashed and left to the local graffiti artists. But one of my team, Jinesh, spent many months tracking down the owners. Now, having completely refurbished the site, we've been here for more than seven years.

We also have premises in nearby Elstree, but are looking for a large piece of land to purchase for a permanent base. It's a lot of hassle to move everything, especially with all the vehicles and equipment we own. An inventory that began and ended with a single trowel did have some advantages!

14

New Challenges

Every business has to have some form of contingency plan to maintain continuity if an unexpected crisis emerges. We had ours in place, but I don't think anything could have prepared us for the shocking emergence of Covid 19, and the sudden lockdown that was imposed by the government on March 26, 2020.

It presented us all with a very big challenge, professionally and personally. At its peak, Covid was an extremely concerning situation for our colleagues and families – not least because there was so much that was unknown and the fear factors were very high.

In the UK, there was panic for the first three weeks. We witnessed supermarkets being stripped of toilet rolls, rice, pasta and other items that people felt the need to stock their cupboards with. We shut down our main office while we assessed the new situation, and worked out how best to deal with all the new problems.

We immediately set up a risk-assessment team, who came up with a comprehensive set of guidelines and instructions. These included social distancing on sites and in the office, enhanced cleaning and – of course – ordering PPE and masks.

Our protocols helped us to reopen quickly, albeit with far fewer people working together at any one time. It was a very strange and eerie atmosphere at first, but we adapted, focusing our minds on delivering as best as we could for our clients.

Initially, it was actually very useful as the streets were empty when the lockdowns were in place. This gave us a greater freedom to work on the different projects. However, people who were at home soon began complaining about the noise if there were works near to where they lived. We had to set up a public relations team to liaise with the residents, keeping them informed when we were in their area.

As the weeks turned into months, we found that some people who were forced to stay indoors were really struggling with the roadworks. We seemed to become a lightning rod for some of those who were getting very upset with what was happening – even though the wider issues around Covid were a long way out of our control.

We started getting abusive letters and calls. There were even a number of occasions where people threatened to kill themselves if we didn't stop work. That was awful and very difficult to deal with.

We also encountered some practical problems with cars that were being left for long periods on the street, especially in locations such as Slough and Ipswich. These obstacles created a few delays. In London, it is a lot easier to arrange for them to be moved to nearby roads. Here was yet another challenge that we had to start planning for.

Covid also changed the dynamic of our business relationship with some of our clients, especially with cash flow issues cropping up yet again. We'd complete the jobs as per the contract, and on time, but then find that there were very long delays in getting paid. The hold-ups were caused by people working from home.

This new working culture had a massive impact, in a way we hadn't expected. For many months, we often found that extracting even the most basic information from some clients took an unacceptably long time. Their teams were no longer in their office, and lacked access to essential facts.

For example, prior to Covid it was normal practice to bring all the relevant partners together for the main project meeting in an office or at the site. That way, we could all go through the plans, raise concerns, and get all the details that we needed for the job. Suddenly that was all suspended. It was the same with the local authorities, where there was no one working in the highways departments.

Gradually we all adapted, some faster than others, and the almost entirely new concept of video conferencing became incorporated into our daily lives. We hadn't really used apps such as Zoom or Teams before. It was a very strange and unsettling experience at first, but it is now a part of the job – one of the main lasting changes to the way we do business.

Other elements changed as we adapted to the post-Covid world. Some of our own staff are now working from home one day a week, which reduces the environmental impact of travel, while we have become an increasingly paperless environment. Having had the virus in 2021, I would not wish it on anyone. I hope that we won't ever have to go through nationwide lockdowns again.

Despite the scale of the crisis, I did feel that the Government came up with a good response overall. Especially for small and medium-sized businesses that would otherwise have struggled to stay solvent. We had to relinquish some contracts, but were able to use the furlough scheme that was introduced very swiftly by the chancellor of the exchequer, Rishi Sunak. This made sure that all our staff were retained and no-one lost their jobs, which was a big relief.

The feedback I've had from other businesses around Europe suggests that the UK government provided one of the very best support packages in the world. That saved many jobs, and kept businesses such as ours from going to the wall, even though it will take time to pay the funding back and see the economy recover.

Fortunately, we seemed to have learned a lot from the 2008-09 financial crisis. Sunak realised that he had to move very quickly and decisively. He should be praised for putting aside ideology in favour of pragmatism.

I have no doubt that, at the critical point, the measures put in place saved a lot of lives. Many people had mental health problems because of lockdown, but if there had been additional financial pressures on them, a number of them might not be here today.

These past few years have seen us facing one challenge after another. The impact of Brexit was soon followed by the dreadful period of Covid, and then the huge problems with fuel – and driver shortages. We had to cope with supply-chain hold-ups – a constant headache for businesses in our sector – and are now dealing with issues around energy and the cost-of– living rises.

The price of basics such as cement, wood and piping have gone up faster and more dramatically than at any time in my career. Things like that can make life very difficult, as we try to fulfil our contracts on time and in budget.

We've been very fortunate, had some luck, performed some miracles, worked hard, and stayed on top of the details. But sometimes you have to hold up your hands and accept that there is nothing you can do. For example, we needed special grouting that was going to be used on a major infrastructure project.

It had to come from Holland, but the delivery company had a shortage of pallets and drivers, so they were unable to ship them to England at the agreed time. We needed to finish the job, but were unable to do it, and had to renegotiate with the client.

In March 2021, a giant 400m long container ship – the Ever Given – became stuck and completely blocked the Suez Canal. It took more than a week to clear. An estimated 10 billion dollars of trade was held up, as hundreds of vessels had to join long queues at either end of the waterway. The world is now so tightly interconnected that one breakdown can cause chaos. That was a perfect example of the butterfly effect.

It had a direct impact on us, because all our plastic piping was held up on one of the delayed vessels. We urgently needed it to hit a deadline. We searched the internet and found some replacements in Scotland that cost a lot to purchase and transport south, but we had no other option as we couldn't just delay the roadworks. All the permissions and planning were in place and parking permits purchased.

My team did a terrific job, but we took a big financial hit. Part of our challenge was to delay the projects in order to cope. We had to switch things round, and be very flexible by stopping and restarting projects depending on when the essential parts actually arrived.

That period lasted for a couple of months, but even now there are ongoing problems.

But if we are forced to pause for a couple of weeks, it gets messy. Contractors and clients are likely in end up in litigation if they are not able to work together and find ways of overcoming the setbacks.

At times, we can have the staff on site, but be waiting for the materials. If the client won't pay for the delays, I fear a lot of legal battles lie ahead throughout the industry. Costs get passed down the line when everyone tries to renegotiate to reduce the risk.

Logistics is such an important element of a civil engineering business like ours, because when one part gets blocked – even if we have no control – it creates many knock-on problems. We are constantly reviewing our risk assessments and contingency plans as jobs progress.

Another illustration is linked to the ongoing, long-term energy crisis. Hold-ups of up to five months in 2021 meant there were no meters available to be installed in new property developments. We were unable therefore to install the electricity and gas supplies. That in turn had a knock-on effect for the purchasers, and also tied up all our money as we couldn't get a completion certificate until they arrived.

We then had the astonishing cost-of-living crisis which hit everyone's margins and profits and caused even more problems in the supply chains for many businesses around the UK. There were so many factors, including the war in Ukraine, but my priority was to find a way of dealing with the sudden shocking rises in energy costs.

They had a massive impact on the work we were already contracted to carry out and created an uncertainty that was very troubling for many months. I had to ensure that we continued to deliver for our customers and employees whilst also keeping the businesses afloat, but it was not always easy.

That is why we are constantly looking at risk and forecasts, and have changed the way we plan and budget. It's vital that all the staff are onboard and updated about what's going on, so that they understand how important it is for us to achieve our targets.

In this business, we agree fixed costs with clients in advance, so sudden and unexpected price rises can cause us big problems. It certainly wasn't foreseen that inflation would start hitting levels that haven't been seen since the 1970s.

It is up to everyone in the company to look at innovative ways of planning and strategy, communicate that to the chain, and try and improve what we do. I believe that nine times out ten we find a way through. The lesson from all these crises is that the companies which learn to adapt will survive, becoming more efficient and stronger.

When I started out on this business journey, I had no idea how many different areas were required to build and grow a successful company. I suspect that if someone had given me a full breakdown as I sat typing my first invoice all those years ago, I might have looked at doing something else with my life!

I have commitments to my team and our clients and my family, so we will always find a solution – although it is sometimes very tough. Work becomes challenging when it encroaches on my personal and family life.

But I enjoy the whole process of problem-solving. We have excellent employees and a very strong team, so I have every confidence that our businesses will move to the next level by taking on and delivering ever more complex projects.

At the moment, I am fixated on emissions as I don't want to be part of a business which is contributing towards killing people. That comes down to planning and research as well. For example, can we structure things so that we reduce the number of vans we need on each job? Are we able to change our work patterns and finish jobs a few days earlier than we did in the past, thereby reducing emissions?

I always insist that we carefully plan the days we allocate to each job, trying to keep them as low as possible. We now make great use of apps that we have developed ourselves after many years of research and development. These enable us to stay in touch with our teams, and allow us all to instantly share information, ideas and suggestions.

My next goal is to reduce working hours, so the staff have a better work-life balance. I would rather they start and finish earlier, as they are less likely to be caught up in traffic queues, and they will burn less fuel.

It is also important that they all have time to see their families. Being a dad, I know that my kids would like me to spend more time with them, whether that means going to the park or taking the dog out. But if I don't get home until after 7pm, there isn't a lot of time left after dinner. If we can make it work, I'm sure the staff will be happy, and our neighbours near the sites will be pleased. We need to use our time smartly so we are free to enjoy our lives.

15

Giving Back

Despite the difficulties that I've previously mentioned, we have been very fortunate and enjoyed a long and sustained period of growth across our businesses in the UK and Romania. That has enabled us to start giving back to local communities in both countries, and that is something I'd like to increasingly focus on in the coming years.

Our London-based staff often take part in local initiatives such as cleaning and clearing local parks and children's play areas. In Romania, we have built and donated new homes to families who – through no fault of their own – found themselves homeless.

In the UK, we also support many charitable organisations, including those that help look after some of the most vulnerable members of the Romanian community. Especially those who have been trafficked and exploited, or are homeless and jobless and struggling to survive in London.

At the start of 2022, we entered into a new sponsorship partnership with one of the best known and most highly regarded orchestras in the world. I'm talking about the Royal Philharmonic Orchestra, who are about to move to new offices in Wembley, a short walk from my home.

The first part of our sponsorship was to support the pilot phase of their new music academy for Brent, in partnership with many other local organisations. The cross-genre academy will provide a pathway to careers throughout the music industry, from music production and administration to performance in any musical style or genre.

It is hoped that this unique development programme will provide professional-level training across the industry for young people in Brent, regardless of background, prior achievement, financial prosperity or other barriers.

The cause is something very close to my heart because of my background. When I attended the launch of the academy in March 2022, I was reminded of the restrictions of my own childhood – and the story of a girl who wanted to play the violin but was unable to because she lived in a tiny flat. The objections of her parents and neighbours left her with no option but to play in a park.

When we lived in just two rooms, there was no opportunity to learn music or any other art form. Memories of my own childhood underlined why it is so important for us as a family and company to support causes such as this. Through these sorts of initiatives, as many young people as possible can enjoy the opportunity to explore and fulfil their potential.

I'd initially met the RPO's Managing Director James Williams when he invited me and Simona to be his guests at a performance of the orchestra at the Royal Albert Hall to celebrate their 75th anniversary. We had a wonderful evening.

My company had dug up the roads outside the famous old venue, but this was the first time we'd ever set foot inside it. The experience was very special.

It is very important to me that I always continue to learn and progress, whether that is for my own benefit or for my family and my business. I see our involvement with the RPO as a chance to discover new music, meet different people, and grow as a person. It is an amazing opportunity.

One unexpected bonus of our sponsorship came when Simona and I were invited to a very special dinner at Windsor Castle on March 29, 2022, to celebrate the 75th anniversary of the orchestra being founded by Sir Thomas Beecham.

It was hosted by their patron, HRH the Prince of Wales. This was an astonishing experience – not only to be shown around the historic 1000-year old building, but also to meet supporters of the orchestra who had travelled from all parts of the world to attend.

Phones and cameras were not allowed to be taken into the venue, so we have to rely on our memories. But what wonderful memories they are, especially of the conversation we had with the then Prince Charles who is a big supporter of Romania and has been there on a number of occasions. I told him that I suspected I was the only person in the room who had previously dug up the road outside Buckingham Palace!

We had the additional privilege of being seated in the front row with Prince Charles as the assembled guests listened to a special performance of the orchestra. As I looked around me and took in the beautiful music, I reflected on the journey I had been on from that small village in Bukovina.

Just five months after that magical evening in Windsor Castle, the man we were privileged to meet and spend time with is now King Charles III, which makes the memories even more special.

The strange thing is that, even when I was digging holes in the ground, I always felt that one day these things would happen. I've always believed that hard work, determination and a positive attitude can bring rewards, especially in the UK, and I hope that is a message all young Romanians can take inspiration from.

When I first arrived in this country in 2007, I already had a strong belief that one day I would have my own company and staff and logo. For some reason I never doubted that I would get there.

But I also believe very strongly that it is important to have a vision. You need to look ahead and ask yourself what your goals are. How will you get there? How committed are you to always learn and adapt? Will you seek out new experiences, innovations and people? Will you find new ways of doing things? What can you imagine?

It is essential to believe in yourself and to try lots of things, but not to get disheartened if they don't all work. As I mentioned earlier in the book, I have always loved boxing. Like a boxer, when things don't go well you have to do as they do.

That means getting back up, dusting yourself down, developing a new strategy and starting again. No one achieves success without first experiencing failure, because that is how we learn. There may be short-term pain, but the long-term gain is worth it.

You also have to overcome your ego, and accept there is always more that can be learned. It is important to have people in your circle who will question you. Ideally, you need someone who will sometimes say no, and who has life and business experiences that are very different to yours.

I have learned that it is not good for my business if I only have yes men around me. It is crucial to hear alternative views. If you encourage people to feel they can speak honestly and openly, you will improve your own understanding of life.

I have also discovered that, as you become successful, there are an increasing number of people who want to use and exploit you. So it is good to have trusted friends and colleagues to look out for that, and to flag up any potential dangers that you may have missed.

16

Romania Today

As I began this book with a look back at how far Romania was behind the rest of Europe when I was a child, it seems appropriate to finish with a few thoughts about how things are now. I visit very regularly to see my mum and other family members – and because I need to keep an eye on my various business interests. It is certainly true that many things have improved in Bukovina.

People who live in the area where I grew up now have far greater choice in all the basics of life. Their homes are full of modern appliances, while the internet offers access to the rest of the world. The downside, however, is that so many young people have left their villages to move to other countries for work and family life. That is building up a big potential problem for the future, as many rural areas are being left with ageing populations and not enough young people to support them.

Because of the systemic corruption and inertia that still dominates so much of Romanian politics, it often seems as if the people working in the diaspora are the only ones keeping the country going. Collectively, we send billions of pounds back home to support our families and friends.

Much of the infrastructure has been sold off or destroyed. It is heart-breaking to see so many legislators who still appear to be in politics for themselves. There is a sickness of the mind in much of Romania that seems unable to break away from the mentalities of the past.

I was recently speaking with an entrepreneur who had worked in Italy but decided to open some garages in Romania. He was puzzled to discover that, in one of them, numerous screwdrivers kept disappearing. So he installed CCTV and found that one of the older employees, who had grown up under Ceausescu, was stealing them one at a time.

He went to speak to the man at his home, and discovered he had boxes full of the screwdrivers. My friend was astonished when the thief apologised, and explained he'd taken them just in case he needed them one day in the future and there was a shortage. That sums up the approach many still have, and the level of thinking that still needs to be tackled.

There has been some change – but the improvement remains marginal. It is one of the reasons I left the country. I realised at an early age that if you don't have the money, or know someone well connected in authority, there is little you can do to succeed on your own. Corruption is endemic at every single level. Decision-making processes are still painfully slow because of the astonishing levels of red tape.

In some ways, as controversial as this may sound, I think Ceausescu actually had some good overall visions for the country. But it was the people around him who were dominant. They kept him in the dark. I remember that my dad used to claim that the president was increasingly manipulated by the secret service as he grew older.

When an official visit to a village was announced, the local administrators knew well in advance. They had time to make everything seem impressive, which meant lots of food in the shops, and the fields looking full so that Ceausescu probably never really understood what was happening.

He didn't know the reality as everything was whisked away after he left, and he was under the impression that all was perfect. So when people started shouting and rallying against him at the time of the revolution, he was shocked and seemed almost like a mediaeval ruler who had been protected from the truth. He may have genuinely thought the people had everything they wanted: houses, jobs and money. He couldn't understand why they were so angry.

But there is also so much to celebrate in the people, culture, landscape and tradition we have in Romania. We have never fought a war against any nation to gain anything. We only fight to defend ourselves, and that has sometimes meant that we've not had opportunities to create or understand our own identity.

Looking from a distance, it seems as though Romania is almost untouched and unknown. It is definitely untapped. And that is something we should all work to change, as the possibilities are enormous.

Throughout the centuries, there have been many fluctuations in rulers and identity. As a country, we sometimes lack a sense of self. But the stunning mountains, plentiful rivers, beautiful Black Sea coast and historic cities are waiting to be explored by visitors as well as returning ex-pats.

Romania would have great potential and opportunities if it could think more like British people do. Especially because of its geopolitical location. In the past it has often been seen as a buffer between the East and West, but how much better would it be if we reversed that attituded and instead viewed ourselves as a bridge? With the right leadership, it could offer great things to the UK and to Europe.

I know there is a strong tradition in the UK of towns and cities twinning with others in countries around the world. Perhaps I should take that to another level and propose that we actually twin Britain and Romania themselves!

It does, however, still feel that people are not doing enough to become involved with local politics and regional management. That is something that really needs to change. I always feel emotional when I return home and find that many parts of the local economy are even worse than when I was a child.

At least back then there were several small factories which employed villagers in the forest industry. Those are now gone, and have been replaced by massive companies which bring in the plant, process the wood, and destroy the work in the villages. As a result, the next generation will have lost all the knowledge and experience of the past ones.

We all know that Romania needs an honest, practical and dispassionate leadership. Politicians who look at what needs to be done now, and plan for the future, rather than forever fighting the same old battles of the past. Especially as a lot of the things we were told when we were young have turned out to be lies and distortions. Or, as disinformation is now more commonly described, fake news.

I'd like to become involved in Romanian politics at the right time, because I feel it is important that those of us who left should try to improve the lives of people in our homeland. I knew I had to leave because there was no hope or opportunity for me at that time. But there is now talk of some eight or nine million in the Romanian diaspora, which is an extraordinary number.

Many of those I speak to say they would like to return home if there was a better system of leadership, and if they could genuinely trust the democratic process. So it is a tragedy that they are not confident to risk moving their businesses and families back.

Romania is suffocating itself because of the relentless stories and allegations of everyday corruption, the need to have the right contacts for contracts, and the backhanders that have to be paid at every level to get jobs done. It often seems to be a democracy in name only.

There are a lot of hard-working and intelligent people who prefer to stay in the shadows at the moment. Because of the fear that is left over from the Ceausescu era, good people tend not to come forward. Which allows the bad people to set the agenda and take advantage.

When I stood in 2020 as a candidate for the Romanian Senate, I came across so many talented people. They were working in diverse fields as doctors, writers, engineers, scientists, and so on. But they are now based in countries such as Canada, Italy, Germany, the USA and Spain. These are genuinely good people who felt they had to leave Romania so they could support themselves and their families, but so many want to return or contribute in other ways.

For the Romanians who chose to move to the UK, where they are now settled with homes, jobs and families, I think it is very important that they become as integrated as possible. It's valuable to have a British passport, so you can enjoy the benefits of dual nationality, learn English, become part of the British way of life, and register to vote.

I passionately believe that it is an important civic duty for us to all vote in local and national elections. During the 2022 local elections in London, I worked hard on social media, and also knocking on doors. I wanted to meet our community and encourage them to register, vote, and be a part of the decision-making process.

I'm aware that a deep distrust of the political system in Romania has inevitably led to some of that feeling remaining with those who have moved to the UK. But it is essential that we all have a say in scrutinising local policy and elected representatives. Which can only happen if we exercise our democratic rights.

As a Romanian who wishes to encourage long-term change at home, I feel that there is much we can learn from the good parts of the UK system. I want to observe British political life as closely as possible. But perhaps the biggest challenge the diaspora has is that it is so divided.

We lack leadership, not least because we are spread across so many nations. We need to find a way to work together and stop dividing the Romanian communities. We need genuine leaders, not fake ones who are looking for fame and finance.

We also have to be very honest about problems in our own culture and communities. I am thinking in particular about human trafficking.

I know from my own experiences when I moved here that homes are sometimes shared by many people at a time in an attempt to save money. They then stick with the people they know and can understand, which often prevents integration with other communities. That in turn can lead to great pressures building up.

It is a big issue that we need to address. One way of doing that is by education and helping to inform more people in our community about the help that is available from the government, and many excellent charities here in the UK.

These are all part of the reasons why I have tried to involve myself in politics. I want to help our community, as well as the wider one, but also to learn about the democratic process as it is so different to that of Romania. Registration, voting, ballot boxes and simple things like placing an X against a name in secret can be so empowering.

I have now stood in three elections and unfortunately not been elected, but I am encouraged rather than disheartened, which is why I am standing for the London Assembly as a Conservative Party candidate in May 2024. I still have a lot to learn and I am eager to pick up as much as possible. It is going to take time, and I will find that my thoughts are not always the right ones. But I'm willing to discover new ideas and processes. I want to work out what could help the people of Romania as we move through the 21st Century.

Writing this book reminds me where I came from. It has given me a clearer picture of my past and how it has impacted on where I am now. I feel like reliving my personal history has helped prepare me for the next stage of my life, which still has many surprises in store. It is a very different experience when someone who is used to flying a small plane is then handed a large one, but I'm willing to commit to doing that.

I hope that any future political career I might have will reflect the sentiments and aspirations expressed in these pages, and help future generations of Romanians to enjoy a free and prosperous future.

It hasn't always been easy to look back at the mistakes I've made, and investments in ventures that didn't work. But I know that all my missteps will help me in the years ahead. I have also realised that I am now more reflective. I look at things differently, and take more time to make decisions.

I've always been spontaneous and instinctive, and reached conclusions based on my gut instinct. But since a friend suggested I try applying the '24-hour rule' of delay and review, I am confident that a new maturity is emerging – as is natural as we grow older. I understand the need to build a legacy, to become a better person, and to put more back into society.

When I visit Bukovina, I get out my quad bike and ride to the places where, 20 years ago, I'd go walking with my dad. When I think back to those days, remembering who I was and where I came from, it's amazing to consider how far I have reached. Yet I'm still nowhere near achieving my full potential.

I always see myself as being in transition from a poor working-class boy to an established businessman – and maybe now something more. I am grateful to be a part of the first generation of Romanians who had a chance to move up a level, become wealthier, develop a business, and provide those who come after us with everything they need: a better education, more life opportunities and greater security.

Mum is still in our family home in Cârlibaba. My brother and I have been renovating the house for her so she will always be comfortable and secure, which is no more than she deserves after the struggles of her early and married life.

To make sure she also has an independent income, I'm planning to build a small hotel on some ground we purchased next door. With the assistance of staff, she will run that when it opens. It has been another challenge. We first had to ensure there is proper drainage, which involved a lot of digging as so much water comes down from the mountains. But all seems to be going well, and I hope it will also bring some new tourists into the region.

I also hope that my story shows it is possible to emerge happily from adversity or poverty. There are often unexpected opportunities for those who are prepared to make a change, celebrate randomness, and create something different for themselves.

Of course, I also realise that this is not possible for everyone. That is why I believe it is equally important for those of us who have been fortunate enough to enjoy some success to share it with others. Which is why our businesses will be increasingly involved in charitable projects. I hope that we will be able to assist a lot of people in Romania and the UK in the coming years.

17

Reflections and the Future

I thought I'd write this book partly in the hope that my story might inspire some other young people who have grown up in poverty, or with difficult backgrounds – especially Romanians. I wanted to show them that it is possible to make big changes, take control of your own life, and build a successful business. You just have to imagine, to believe in yourself and your dream and to then take the appropriate actions. I. B. A. Imagination. Belief. Action.

The greatest football manager of all time, Sir Alex Ferguson, was born and brought up in a very rough and poor part of a city I earlier mentioned that I had once accidentally briefly visited – Glasgow. He went on to manage Manchester United to 13 Premier League titles as well as winning the FA Cup five times and the UEFA Champions League in 1999 and 2008.

In his 2013 autobiography, he wrote *'It's precisely because I started out in the shipbuilding district of Glasgow that I achieved what I did in football. Origins should never be a barrier to success. A modest start in life can be a help more than a hindrance.'*

Those words are particularly relevant to Romania, as there is so much untapped potential within the population. Romanian citizens deserve every opportunity to grow, learn, flourish, and create great lifestyles for themselves and their families.

But during the writing process I have also learned a lot about myself. This is the first time I've ever taken a moment to look in depth at my past, to examine my decisions, and to consider how and why I've lived my life this way. I have come to realise how much I rush everything, that I always have to be doing something, and that I very rarely relax.

I don't seem to have time to read many papers, so I get all my news online or from social media. I'm not sure if that is entirely healthy. Other than when I'm at the gym, I never listen to music or podcasts, or even watch much TV. That is something I'd like to change.

As I mentioned earlier, it was incredible when Simona and I were kindly invited to the Royal Albert Hall as guests of the Royal Philharmonic Orchestra. And yet, typically, the first thing I did when we arrived outside the venue was to spot the barriers of a rival civil engineering contractor on a nearby road.

I rushed straight over to see how they had left their site at the end of the day. I was not impressed. Neither was Simona. She told me very firmly that it was time to turn off and just relax, but it is not always easy.

I have so much drive and commitment and always get up early, no matter what I did the night before or how I feel, because I want to. I love it. I enjoy working and the daily challenges. And, of course, I enjoy providing for my family. I always want to make sure that they will never have to endure the privations that my siblings and I suffered when we were children

I believe I'm very fortunate to have been part of the first generation of businessmen to have access to new tools such as Google and YouTube. These have been a great substitute for those of us who were unable to go to university or be apprentices. It is a new way of learning compared to earlier times, but it means that we can often find a wide range of solutions very quickly.

Now I want to get out and see more of the world, the UK, and London – but from ground level and inside the historic buildings rather than from beneath them. The irony is that I know what is under the roads. I know what holds London up and how fragile it is, because being under the ground you see things no-one else does.

Perhaps I need to slow down, but maybe that is also just my way and I will never change. As I look back through these pages, I see that – whether it was with my marriage or my business – my approach has always been quick, quick, quick.

When you put everything in writing, you suddenly see the patterns. I think I was always afraid I would miss out if I didn't do things straight away. I like to make quick decisions, but overall it seems to have worked out reasonably well from a business and family point of few.

I don't think I could have discovered a better wife, and

that was my best quick decision of all. Simona cares not only about our business but also about me, our children and our wider family. This is a great thing to have in a partner. I love and value the fact that she is always alongside me.

Maybe if we had known each other better, we wouldn't have got married. But it was an instinctive decision to propose. Later on, we discovered new things about each other's personalities and habits, as every couple does. But by then we were married and then came the children, so we had to adapt all the time, and we still do.

In fact, since I began the process of researching and writing this book, we were blessed with a fourth child! Miriam completed our family line-up when she was born in May 2023, so now we have two boys and two girls.

Sport is probably the one area that still helps me to relax. I love doing exercise as I've always found it to be the most effective way to disconnect. After the near-fatal assault in Portugal, it was sport that gave me that breathing space to carry on and be relaxed. If I don't do exercise, I can easily lose my drive and motivation. The training sharpens me up and makes me relaxed, even if I just run for a couple of hours.

That is one of the reasons why I installed the gym at work. I always wanted the staff to have the facilities to exercise, as I know the benefits it can provide. It has certainly improved some of their health issues, and that ultimately benefits the business as well as themselves and their wellbeing.

My heroes in life tend to come from sport as well. I'm thinking of people like Mike Tyson, for what he achieved in the ring after his own terrible background and childhood.

Or Nadia Comaneci, who made Romanians so proud. Or Cristiano Ronaldo for his dedication. Ronaldo isn't just one of the best footballers of all time; he is becoming a brilliant businessman as well.

We are now in the process of setting up a new Corporate Social Responsibility programme across the range of our businesses in Romania and the UK. We are passionate about sharing some of our success and helping others also achieve their own dreams. I'm also studying Theology, taking a correspondence degree course. I'm now on year three, so I hope to complete my delayed exams and then decide which other directions I'd like my life to go in, with politics being one possible option.

I also hope this book and my story might help inspire others and open their minds to what might be possible. If I had been able to read such a book when I was young, I think it would have helped me to develop my approach to life. I always considered myself to be an outsider. I realised when I moved to Western Europe that I often saw things very differently to many of those I met, because of the childhood I'd had.

I was a poor person with a big dream but without a road-map. Perhaps this book may at least give a few tips and ideas to others who are looking at their own next stages in life. I have always known that I want to be the best I possibly can. That I want to seek out the best opportunities, create the best jobs, and drive for better outcomes while also trying to be fair and straight.

I like people to enjoy their work but also to take responsibility for what they do. When I engage in something, I put everything of myself into the project. I work hard and just want to get it done well. I have gathered some very good people around me. It isn't always easy, but I've learned that when you find these gems, it is important to treat them well so you can collectively build together.

Someone said '*You learn until you die, and even when you die you haven't learned everything.*' So I will try to learn as much as I can, by speaking to the right people who are relevant to each situation I face. Never be afraid to ask advice or seek new knowledge. That is one of the biggest tips I can pass on to my children.

I get many people contacting me on social media asking how I have managed so far. So I hope that some of the things I've written about will be useful – although it is important to remember that every single person will find their own route in their own way. I don't think there is any great secret to success. Be honest, be straight, be a hard worker, listen to others, treat people well, and you will get there.

I thank you for reading this book and give thanks to God for helping me to meet Simona as she is my wife, best friend, business partner and soulmate. And for introducing me to our four beautiful children. The next stage of the adventure now begins and a part of that has been my decision to add the word Bucovineanul to my name as I want to represent the Bukovina region that means so much to my family. I hope my dad would be proud.